Jump

ALSO BY STEVE HARVEY

Act Like a Success, Think Like a Success

Straight Talk, No Chaser

Act Like a Lady, Think Like a Man

Jump

Take the Leap of Faith to Achieve Your Life of Abundance

Steve Harvey
with Leah Lakins

HARPER LUXE

An Imprint of HarperCollinsPublishers

HarperCollins books may be purchased for educational, business, or sales promotional use. For information please e-mail the Special Markets Department at SPsales@harpercollins.com.

FIRST HARPERLUXE EDITION

ISBN: 978-0-06-249695-9

HarperLuxe™ is a trademark of HarperCollins Publishers.

Library of Congress Cataloging-in-Publication Data is available upon request.

16 17 18 19 20   ID/LSC   10 9 8 7 6 5 4 3 2 1

This book is dedicated to all seven of my children—
Brandi, Karli, Morgan, Broderick, Jason, Lori, and
Wynton—whom I love beyond any words. My hope
for you has always been that you live the life of your
dreams. I have tried to set an example; to live by
principles that could be modeled and referenced. It
seems that all of you are willing to jump—and to
accept your share of lumps and bruises along the way.
Marjorie and I are proud of the fact that all of you are
finding your own way. I hope that after I am long gone
that I will have lived a life that will encourage you to
teach your children and grandchildren the importance
of taking the jump. I love you all and thank you for
inspiring me. You have made me a better man, husband,
and father. Without you I would not be possible.
Thank you, all. I love you, and never forget that.

Contents

Invictus

Out of the night that covers me,
   Black as the pit from pole to pole,
I thank whatever gods may be
   For my unconquerable soul.

In the fell clutch of circumstance
   I have not winced nor cried aloud.
Under the bludgeonings of chance
   My head is bloody, but unbowed.

Beyond this place of wrath and tears
   Looms but the Horror of the shade,
And yet the menace of the years
   Finds and shall find me unafraid.

It matters not how strait the gate,
   How charged with punishments the scroll,
I am the master of my fate,
   I am the captain of my soul.

—WILLIAM ERNEST HENLEY

Introduction: Jump

January 13, 2016
***Family Feud Studios*, Atlanta, Georgia**

I would like to share with you these words that I left my studio audience with at the end of a taping of *Family Feud*. I was amazed at the impact these words have had—I have never seen a video of anything I've done go viral so quickly. Fifty-eight million people viewed it! That explosive and immediate response showed me that untold numbers of people around the world are looking for the answers to a better life.

I'm going to tell you something that every successful person in this world has done in his or her life or career. Every successful person has jumped! They have taken their hopes and dreams and took a leap of faith toward them. If you desire greatness in your life, eventually you are going to have to jump. You cannot just exist in this life and automatically find happiness. You have to live every moment to the fullest to achieve a life of abundance. If you are waking up thinking that there is more to your life than there is, *believe* that there is. You have to truly believe in your heart that there is. But in order to get to that life of happiness and abundance, you are going to have to jump.

When God created all of us, He gave every last one of us a gift. He never created a soul without endowing that person with a gift. Please don't think of your gift as only a talent in running, jumping, singing, or dancing. It's more than that. If you know how to network, if you can connect dots, if you draw, if you teach, if you fry chicken better than anyone else, if you can bake pies, if you can cut hair, if you can color hair, or if you can cut grass, that is your gift.

I had a partner who never wanted to hang out late. Me and my friends would say to him, "Man, let's hang out." He would say, "Nah, I have to get up and cut Mrs. Johnson's grass." We kept laughing at this dude for just wanting to cut grass. He now has a landscaping company in Cleveland worth $4 million. All he does is cut grass. But he was gifted at it. I got another partner who owns a detail shop making $800,000 per year. All he does is detail cars, and he has built it into a six-mobile-truck business where he comes to you and details your car. That's his gift and that's what he loves to do. Identify your gift!

Imagine you are standing on the cliff of life and you see people soaring by, going to exotic places—or maybe your neighbor up the street purchases a new car every two years, and you think, "How does he do that?" At those moments, did you ever stop and think, "Maybe this person has identified his gift" or "Maybe he is living in his gift"? Your Bible says, "Your gift will make room for you." It says *your gift*, not *your education*. I know a lot of people who have degrees that they are not using. You can go and get an education. Of course you want to be educated, but your education will take you only so far.

The only way for you to soar is for you to jump. You have to take that gift that is packed away in your backpack, jump off the cliff, and pull the cord.

If you don't ever use it, you are going to become strictly a worker. Your days will become routine. And hopefully you'll have enough money to pay your bills. Is this how you want to live? If you are getting up every morning and going to a job that you hate, that is not living. You're just existing. At some point, you have to see what living is like. The only way you are going to see what living is like is to jump.

When you first jump, your parachute will not open right away. I wish I could tell you that it would, but it won't. You're going to hit some rocks. You're going to get some skin torn off scraping against those cliffs. You may even get parts of your clothes torn off. You will get some cuts and possibly bleed pretty bad. But eventually the parachute will open. That is a promise from God. It is not a theory—it's a promise. Can you name one thing that God has not gotten you through? I sincerely doubt it, because if He hasn't gotten you through it already, He is currently pulling you through it right now. You are the living proof of it, because you are breathing. If He had not gotten you through it, you wouldn't even be here. I guarantee that your parachute will open. But you have to jump and find out for yourself how far you will soar.

You can stand on that cliff of life and be forever safe. You can avoid the cuts and tears. If you don't jump, I have another promise: Your parachute will never open. You'll never know what greatness God really has in store for you. He has promised a wonderful life for you. Your Bible says that He comes to give you life and life more abundantly. If I were you, I would jump. That's the only way to get to that abundant life. You have to jump. You have got to take a chance, or you'll have more of the same.

After you hear these words, and you leave this building, there are those of you who will later discuss them in the car and say, "Well, I got bills. I can't afford to take a leap of faith toward my dream life." Whether you stay on the cliff or you jump, you are going to have bills. Some of you might say, "If I quit my job, I'm going to ruin my credit." If you just have a job, you are just living check-to-check anyway. So, even if you have A1 credit, you probably do not have enough money to live meaningfully.

I completely encourage you to see what God will manifest in your life. If you jump, trust me, God will hold you up. He didn't bring you this far to let you fall. Before you leave this earth, before you die, do yourself a favor—just jump one time.

I can't go anywhere now without someone coming up and telling me how much the Jump video has meant to them. An owner of a golf course came up to me and said, "I now make all the young caddies at my club watch this video every morning. I don't want them to settle for just being a caddy. I want them to know that they can have more." A father stopped me in the airport and said, "I have six kids and I made all of them watch your video. You said exactly what I've been trying to tell them for years."

Jumping is taking a risk, a leap of faith toward your dreams. Jumping is making a major career move. Jumping is rectifying an issue in your personal relationships. Jumping is embracing the ambition that God has put in your imagination, and you making a commitment to manifest it in your life.

What do you see in your imagination? Do you see a new car sitting in your driveway? Can you see that new house you've always wanted? Do you see yourself starting a business? Do you see the man or woman of your dreams? Do you see yourself earning your degree? Can you see your children going off to college? Can you see leaving your high-pressure corporate job to open a food truck? Can you see leaving the cold climate that hampers your health for a warmer one? Can you see adopting a child or being a foster parent? Whatever is in your imagination, God put it there for a reason. The way that you can achieve your vision is to jump.

What you see in your imagination is tied to your gift. As I explained in my previous book, *Act Like a Success, Think Like a Success*, your gift is the thing that you do the absolute best with the least amount of effort. Discovering your gift and how God wants to use your life is the true purpose and power of jumping. God wants you to have the life that you are dreaming about, or else He would not have planted it in your mind. He did not place you on this earth to struggle and do without. He wants you to have your heart's desires. Your willingness to jump will open doors for you. Every jump will increase your wisdom and broaden your vision. The abundant life that God has in store for you will allow you to have unimagined riches; riches so overflowing that you'll have plenty—especially to share with others.

Your willingness to jump will open doors for you. Every jump will increase your wisdom and broaden your vision. The abundant life that God has in store for you will allow you to have unimagined riches; riches so overflowing that you'll have plenty—especially to share with others.

The jumps I have mentioned so far are big jumps. Smaller jumps will enhance your life as well, such as quitting smoking, adding a workout regimen to your schedule, upgrading your look, deciding to speak up more often in professional settings, taking care of your health, getting organized, decluttering, and the like. The smaller jumps can complement your big-picture jump.

Some of us are scared to take the jump. We're fearful because we don't know how it will turn out. Guess what? Every day you wake up, you don't know how it will work out. That's the exciting part about life. And if every day you don't feel excited to start your day, you definitely need to jump. Don't think for a moment that successful people don't have fears. I have fear in my life, especially since I have a family and a business, and I have to watch out for more than just myself. But I embrace fear, because for me it is an indicator that God is calling me to do something bigger. In other words, my faith calms my fears. I have no fears greater than my dreams. Acknowledge your fear and move forward. Fear is there to let you know that what you are taking on is worth your risking your current lifestyle.

Once you jump, God will take it from there. He will place you in positions to learn important lessons that will prepare you for the next stage of your life—your next jump. He will also reward you with abundant blessings along your journey. Knowing that, why wouldn't you jump?

I would not tell you to jump, to take a leap of faith, or to risk where you are now if I hadn't already taken multiple major jumps in my own life. God gave me a vision for my life, and that was to be on television. In order for me to get there, my journey included flunking out of college, being laid off from my job, being homeless for three years, going through two divorces, and owing the IRS tons of money because of horrible advice. In dealing with each one of these setbacks, I chose to jump. And I have kept jumping. Leaving a dead-end job to go on the road as a comedian wasn't about taking a blind risk; it was a leap necessary for me ultimately to live the abundant life that God wanted for me. Now there aren't enough hours in the day for me to walk through every door that God opens. The only way for you to have an abundant life is for you to rise up off those cliffs and keep jumping.

Everybody I know says they want to be happy and they want to be successful. The only difference between you and the successful people you see in your life every day is that they have jumped. You're the only one who can take your dreams off the shelf and turn them into reality. You are the only one who can take *I can't* and turn it into *I can*. You can sit there and watch the years roll by with your dreams unfulfilled, or you can take a chance and live like you've never lived before.

Jump is a testament to what God has done in my life and what I strongly believe that He can do in yours. If I can go from living out of my car to being on television, there's no telling what God has in store for you. Your life should be more than living paycheck-to-paycheck and then hoping to collect a pension down the road. There's no security in putting your life and your dreams in someone else's hands. Your destiny belongs to you. If you are not happy, what are you waiting for? Your life will unfold only when you choose to make that jump.

You don't have to wait until you get your credit together to jump. You don't have to lose ten pounds to jump. You don't have to wait until your children finish school to jump. I guarantee you that your children will be more proud of you when you live a life that makes you happy. Stop waiting for the perfect time. The perfect time to jump is always now. The best day to take on your new life is today. There are people lying in their graves who wished they'd had just one more day to use the gifts they had. If you are able-bodied and breathing, that means that God has more for you. Even when you try something for the first, second, third, or even fourth time and it doesn't work out just how you planned it, you have to keep jumping. God allows for second chances every day. When are you going to stop waiting to take yours?

There is an abundant life waiting for you. The career you've been dreaming about is on the other side of your jump. The big mansion that you've always wanted will come if you jump. The doors of that business you've always wanted will open when you take that jump. There's only one way you're going to get to that life that God has for you—you have to *JUMP.*

Dear Reader: If you'd like to view the Jump video, visit me on Facebook, follow me on Twitter (@IAmSteveHarvey), or watch it on YouTube.

For information on joining the free #JumpWithSteve Success Club, turn to the back of the book.

1

Ain't No Lesson Like a Bought Lesson

Be optimistic when going through adversity.

Adversity is necessary to identify your dream.

There are lessons in failure. There's no such thing as complete failure.

If you accept that life is a series of ups and downs, you will get through the downs.

During adversity is not the time to lick your wounds. Failures make you who you are.

My mother taught my father, who had a third-grade education, how to read and write. He worked for a construction company. Often my brothers and I helped my father at his construction site. But working all day with my hands, doing backbreaking labor, sometimes outside in the hot sun or the freezing cold, wasn't for me.

When I was not working or going to school, I would hang with my boys—Ricardo, Manny, Butch, EL, Lil' John, Gil, and Biggy Wigg. We'd gone to the same schools: Parkwood grade school, then Glenville High. When Ricardo said they were going to Kent State, I decided that I'd go, too, and I applied.

When I told my mother that I wanted to go to college, she said, "Baby, you're going to be something." Her vote of confidence meant everything to me. It was a big deal for me to be accepted to Kent State. I was the first person in my family to go to college.

Attending Kent was cool. I had never lived away from home, and being around a group of people who didn't look like me exposed me to new things. I had a lot of great experiences and learned that the world was bigger than 112th Street in Cleveland.

One day, I was home for a visit. My mother called me into the kitchen and sat me down at the table. She read a letter to me from my school. I had flunked out of Kent State University. It took me completely by surprise. I was on academic probation, but I didn't think they were going to put me out just like that! My routine was to drop a class if I was not performing well, to avoid failing. It turned out that in doing so, I had not accumulated enough credits. I sat there with my mother crying.

I'm telling you this story because if you don't know already, you'll soon learn that life can be a four-letter word. You can be cruising along one day with everything going well, and then the next day you lose your job, you find out that you have a serious health problem, you get evicted, or you unexpectedly lose a loved one. It's just a part of life. There's no way you're going to make it out of this world without spending some time down in the valley or in a dark place. But this isn't the time to give up. This is the time to understand that God is trying to lead you to your purpose and to your gift. Use adversity to your advantage. Don't let it stop you. Instead, allow it to take you to the next level. Allow it to teach you the things you need to know to take you to the next level.

My father always said, "Ain't no lesson like a bought lesson." I was nineteen and had failed big-time in flunking out. A lot of my peers at school wrote me off. One guy said, "Man, you don't know how to finish noth-

---

There's no way you're going to make it out of this world without spending some time down in the valley or in a dark place. But this isn't the time to give up. This is the time to understand that God is trying to lead you to your purpose and to your gift.

---

ing." And some others made it clear that they thought I wouldn't amount to much. It was tough to be hit with a failure like that so early in adulthood. If I had not been careful, it could have defined the rest of my life.

The thing about me, though, is that I immediately try to find the one glimmer of light in the darkness. No matter what happens to me, there has got to be a glimmer of light. I may not see it right away, but I am ever optimistic. I interpreted my situation as, "I failed at college—there must be a reason. What can I learn from this? What can I gain from this?"

I don't know any successful people who haven't failed. They probably wouldn't be who they are or where they are without those failures. Failures make you who you are; they show you what you can overcome. They help you believe in yourself. During adversity is not the time to sit there and lick your wounds. Don't give up on your dream; accept that life is a series of ups and downs and that you will overcome the obstacles.

When successful people are going through adversity, they quickly put it in their rearview mirror and reframe the story. Let's consider a resignation: Behind the scenes, two business partners don't see eye to eye on how to run their operations. The infighting is tearing the company apart. One person decides to leave.

Here's how he may choose to frame it: "I have spent twenty wonderful years working with Bob, who has a great business mind. I have learned a great deal from working for this impressive organization and from Bob's astute business practices. However, I have decided to move on to a new company and bring along all of my invaluable years of experience."

Leave adversity in the past by putting it in your rearview mirror. Reframe your story by looking at the positives. Don't complain that Bob did you wrong; instead, concentrate on all that you've learned at the company and the ways you are going to use that knowledge to move forward. The windshield on your car is big. The rearview mirror is small. There is a reason for that, because you can't drive your car forward looking in the rearview mirror. You will crash! Use your windshield for your big dreams, for the vision of your life moving forward.

When I left Kent State, I did my best not to let that failure stop me from moving toward my future. I still believed that I had many options. I had a roof over my head, and my parents were there for me.

I jumped and got a job at the Ford Motor Company. I started out making $13.50 an hour, and with overtime I made up to as much as $27 an hour. It was 1977 and that was decent money. Ford gave me the opportunity to get a car and help my parents with some bills. So—hold up, partner—I went from being a college student a minute ago making zero to an autoworker making good money!

I think that was one of my first realizations—that struggle and abundance are connected. The struggle comes along with the abundance. It's been my experience that you'll usually enjoy abundance in some form and endure struggle at the same time. Growth is all about struggle and abundance. Every successful person will tell you that with more success comes more responsibility, more struggle, more adversity. So if you expect to have more, to do more, you have to step up. It's a part of the journey.

Deep down, the fact that I was no longer a college student bugged me. It really did, but I kept focusing only on the bright side. I was working and I had some money. Working was positive and something that I could build on. I regularly visited my friends at Kent State on the weekends. I gave my buddies loans, money for gas, books, groceries—whatever they needed. I also took them out to eat. My visits became a ray of light for them. I took my miserable situation and found a glimmer of light.

We were still hanging out, but the difference was that they were able to have fun on the weekends and still do well in school. I watched them progress in their lives. They had their futures mapped out, and I was sitting on the sidelines. I wondered why I was different. Why had I flunked out? It wasn't like we weren't all on the same level intellectually. We'd all been accepted to the school; we'd all been up to the same shenanigans on the weekends. This question troubled me for a while until it dawned on me that my heart simply hadn't been in it. It was clear that I hadn't thought it through. An advertising degree wouldn't have gotten me any closer to my dream of being on television than any job that just supported me would. Going to college wasn't my dream. When I understood this, it became easier for me to put my "failure" in my rearview mirror and to stop focusing on it.

Two years later, my friends were graduating from college. Although I had put the failure behind me, I was still somewhat embarrassed and hurt that I didn't finish my own degree. Even worse, Ford had started laying off workers and shutting down plants. My friends were graduating and I was getting laid off. At that point in my life, I didn't choose to jump. Rather, I was pushed off the cliff without warning. The bright side had turned dark again. I had to try to figure out what to do.

When those lights went out at Ford, it would have been really easy for me to let my mind go to a negative place. What kept me moving forward was the thought "What's next?" After I got laid off from Ford I was willing to try anything. I signed up to sell Amway. Somebody said you can be a diamond distributor. I did that. I sold Dick Gregory's Bahamian Diet. I signed up to sell Shaklee products. A. L. Williams insurance—I sold that, too. If you told me that I could make some money, I went for it. I jumped. I did not care. I was throwing my butt off that cliff in a heartbeat. If I had no idea how to sell soap, it didn't matter. Over and over and over, I repeatedly jumped. It was like jumping into an abyss. I had no idea of the outcome. I jumped merely based on the hope that I could make it. Although I didn't know it at the time, I was open to what God had in store for me. Working at Ford had put some much-needed money in my pocket, but I knew that it wasn't tied to my gift. It was far from what God put me on the planet to do. That moment in the valley was necessary for me to get about the business of owning my life.

It brings to mind a story somebody told me. A young man went to the hospital to visit his grandmother. She was very ill. When he arrived at the hospital, he could clearly see that she wasn't going to make it. He started to cry. His grandmother said, "Baby, I'm getting ready to leave this world."

"Grandma, ain't nothing wrong with you. You're going to be all right."

"No, baby, I'm not going to be leaving this hospital. It's time for me to go," she told him.

He cried and held on to his grandmother a little while longer. Before he left, she asked, "Do you know your great-grandfather's name?"

He said, "No."

"You know why?" she asked. He shook his head.

She said, "Because he didn't leave you nothing. Before you leave this earth, I want you to live your life so that your children's grandchildren will know your name."

This story had a profound impact on my life. I know that God wanted me to hear those words. Her words gave me purpose. Ever since I heard them, my goal in life is to live in such a way that my children's grandchildren will know my name. Her words made me recognize that I have to always dream big and to keep moving forward if I am going to live a life in which I will leave a legacy not only to my children but also to my grandchildren.

As long as God continues to wake you up in the morning, it can't be over. It's never over. (Now, if you're waking up next to the wrong person, you can feel like it's over.) When you're down in the valley, it's time to explore and investigate the possibilities. In every dark moment, you have an opportunity to travel down the hallway of life until you find the right door for you. Even when you get a door slammed in your face, it just means it's time to turn another doorknob, and maybe another, and another. So I put one foot in front of the other, and I took a leap of faith. I jumped to the next thing.

When I got laid off at Ford, thousands of people also lost their jobs at the same time. It showed me that losing my job wasn't about me or my character; it wasn't personal. It was about the economy. If I hadn't lost the job at Ford, I might still be there today and never would have found out what my true gift was, or how much more I could accomplish.

Along your journey, when one door closes, there's always another door you can open. In fact, some of these doors will be slammed in your face by other people. (And it's perfectly normal to want to hit them in the face with the same door. Yes, do it! Just kidding.) Every door isn't for you. You can waste a lot of time wedging your feet in doorjambs or kicking in doors that aren't meant for you.

The doors that God opens for you are not difficult doors to walk through. You can feel when God brings the right things in your life at the right time because it is effortless and smooth sailing. And, suddenly, everybody seems to be encouraging you to pursue the exact same thing God called you to do. Have the courage to walk through the door He has opened especially for you. Do something that pushes you out of your comfort zone. Be willing to jump even when you don't know where you'll land. Your life is a precious gift that is available for a limited time only. At some point, you are going to have to choose to stop living your life in fear and get out on that cliff and step off in faith. Only then will you ever be able to soar.

When you are facing adversity, you can't waste time asking God, "Why me?" Don't let one door slamming in your face keep you from moving on to the next one. Don't let one loss stop you from believing that more is

---

The doors that God opens for you are not difficult doors to walk through. . . . Have the courage to walk through the door He has opened especially for you. . . . Be willing to jump even when you don't know where you'll land. . . . Only then will you ever be able to soar.

---

possible for you. Colonel Sanders opened the first Kentucky Fried Chicken restaurant when he was sixty-two years old. Nobody believed that he could do it. KFC is now the business model for all other chicken franchises. Why? Because he never gave up.

You've got to have a piece of God to hold on to when things get bad. The difficulties you are going through now are actually helping you become the person you need to be later on to appreciate your forthcoming riches. I had to go through every single one of those challenging experiences in my life to turn me into the man I am today. If I hadn't flunked out of Kent State, I might not be where I am today. Graduating with a degree in advertising may not have put me on the road that led to the blessings I have today. Lessons like these have taught me time and time again that nothing worth having is simple or straightforward. You can pick anything that you have gone through or wanted and find the truth in that statement.

I have found that life is a series of setbacks. But a setback can be an opportunity. It can put you in the position to uncover your gift. Setbacks are temporary. There's not a single living soul who will not have to make a comeback after being sidetracked from his or her journey. You may even have to make more than one—or two, or ten!

As you travel through life, you have to believe that God's plan for you is greater than any plan you could ever come up with. But to reach it, you'll have to walk on a road filled with adversity, a road filled with struggle—but also with abundance. Life is going to get bad sometimes. You'll make poor choices. You'll fail. You'll lose hope and maybe want to give up. If you jump, and trust that He will be there to help you soar, there is nothing you cannot achieve.

Believe me, I know how hard it can be to keep your hope alive. I know that it can sometimes be hard to get out of bed to go to a job you don't love, one that doesn't challenge you or even help you pay all your monthly bills. I know what it feels like to be in a relationship or a marriage that isn't right for you, that doesn't sustain you the way you need it to. But can you afford to stay where you are, living day to day without hope or faith? I recommend that you get up and do something that brings you one step closer to being in a better situation. I encourage you to trust in yourself, in your gift, and in God.

When you look at a bad breakup, a failed marriage, or a missed opportunity for a promotion, you have to stop and ask yourself, "Do I really want to spend another year in this situation? Do I really want to stay at a job that refuses to give me the position and salary that

I deserve?" Maybe you shouldn't fight so hard or be disappointed. There is a reason for every disappointment and failure; I see it as the impetus that leads us to bigger and better things. Yes, you can feel down and disappointed; you can be frustrated; you can even take some time to think about your life and where you are going, or where you want to go. But what you can't do is give up. Nothing comes in the package you expect or arrives exactly when you want it to.

Let's say you are a woman who is married to a very successful man, and all of a sudden he says he doesn't want you anymore. He wants a divorce, and you get served papers. You've been standing by this man all these years and you get blindsided with a divorce. Your whole world is crumbling around you. You start taking a dive and you don't know how you are going to recover. Immediately, you address the hurt. You call your girlfriends. You all meet up, talk about it, drink wine, shed a few tears.

As hurt and pain is a part of life, you can't let this moment in the valley take you out. You can't stay there. It might not be easy at first, but try to look on the bright side. Did you really want to stay with someone who doesn't want to be with you? Were you really happy anyway? And since you've been there that whole time standing by him, aren't you entitled to a sizable alimony and perhaps child support? You now have the freedom and resources to go and discover who you really are, because you are free from having to hold him up and keep everything together. Let's find a glimmer of hope in the pain.

I could have let flunking out of college define my aspirations. Instead, I jumped to a job that carried me along for a while and gave me the confidence to do other things. When I lost the Ford job, I was down and depressed, but I see now that it did what I needed it to do. It got me through a hard time after having to leave college.

Make sure that you are open to and available for the greater possibilities in your life, for the bigger blessings. You will never be able to fully enjoy what God has in store for you if you don't get out of bed, or out of your house, or try anything new. You have to be open to new experiences and opportunities. You have to take a chance on yourself. Get out of your coach-seat expectation and get yourself a first-class vision for your goals and your dreams. God has so much more in store for you than what you can see or even imagine right now. Believe in Him, and have faith.

When life knocks you down, don't see it as failing. It's added experience that you now have under your belt. The more experiences you have, the more life currency you earn, which you can use to go out and tackle bigger opportunities with bigger risks for a rewarding outcome. Invaluable experience comes with a price. There are no scholarships in life. There are no rewards in life for just showing up. You pay for it. The bigger the failure, the bigger the cost is. You bought it. It's yours; now you can learn from it.

When you are adding currency to the bank of your life, you won't even realize how much you have banked until life starts hitting you with some closed doors. You won't know until you have to face your hard times how much you have inside yourself to overcome them. Even when you feel like you are about to go into a negative balance, you have to trust that you will never go bankrupt. As long as you are moving forward, there will always be something else you can deposit into the bank of your life.

No mistake bankrupts you for life! Failure isn't final. Failure is simply an experience that has already finished. It's all in how you handle it. It's an opportunity to learn about yourself and to grow. When you are going through adversity, look for the lesson in it. In every single moment of adversity in your life there are lessons to be learned. If you let the adversity crumble you, you will lie there and wallow in the failure, but life is 10 percent what happened and 90 percent what you're going to do about it.

Several years ago, there were a lot of rumors going around about me and my personal life and my business. And the majority of them were flat-out not true. The rumors that were being spread were very damaging, to the point where I had to explain myself to sponsors and the like. It had gotten really ugly for me—both personally and professionally—as well as for my family. Quite naturally, for most of us our instinct is to respond. Because I had a platform, which was my nationally syndicated radio show, I felt like I could have opened up my mic and started blasting back. It was then that my friend Anderson Cooper called.

"Steve, come on my show and I'll help you straighten it out." He had always been very friendly toward me, and he's a great guy.

"OK, cool!"

My appearance on his show was going to be on a Monday night. The Saturday before, I got a call from Tyler Perry. He wanted to know how I was doing given all the rumors. "Hey, buddy, you hanging in there?"

"Nah, man, I'm dying over here. I'm really hurting. I'm in a world of pain. But, it is going to be all right because I'm going on the Anderson Cooper show and straighten this all out. He's giving me a shot to tell my side of it and deflect some of the lies."

"You ain't going on no Anderson Cooper show," said Tyler Perry.

I got quiet for a minute before I spoke. "Tyler, did you hear what I said? This is Anderson Cooper."

Tyler Perry went on to explain: "When they are talking about you—these rumors—it's a blog. When you talk, when you respond, it's a press conference. Sit still and in two weeks it will all go away. The bottom feeders will find something else because they like fresh do-do."

"Alright, man."

The only problem was, it felt like it was more than two weeks. It felt like an eternity. The fire I was in—the hellfire I was in the midst of—felt like an eternity. I was being discussed everywhere—including on YouTube.

I don't listen to many people who haven't been knocked down by life. I don't take a lot of advice from folks who talk a good game but aren't out there on the court of life taking their shots. I recommend seeking advice from people who have traveled the road you've traveled, who have the experience to give you good advice—not people who try to give you advice about things they don't know anything about. They may mean well, but their limited experience could affect you negatively.

With every lesson you learn, you add more confidence and gain more strength for the next part of your journey. But you must determine that the experience was a lesson, not a failure. If you consider the experience a failure, then you lose confidence. A series of failures, losing a bit of confidence each time, will leave you so unsure of yourself that you won't even try to get back in the game. You've got to determine that your experiences are lessons, not failures, not mistakes. Lessons.

If I wasted time addressing everyone who said something negative about me, I would never have time to focus on the real reason God put me here on earth. Every moment you spend addressing a critic is a valuable moment that you take away from your dream.

It makes sense that my life has not been a straight line. My life's been filled with ups and downs, successes and failures, great achievements and deep losses. I have found that in every moment of adversity there is a lesson. The sooner I recognized this, the sooner I put the adversity behind me. Don't make your past mistakes larger by focusing all your attention on them and neglecting to concentrate on your future successes. God has already gotten you through the mistake, so don't keep it in front of you. Life is too short to spin your wheels regretting the choices you've already made. It happened. It's over. Let it be done.

The faster you can get to the bright side, the quicker you can move on with your life toward your lesson. You can't let setbacks, mistakes, or disappointments keep you down or hold you back. You are not the first person who's gotten a divorce. You are not the first person to have lost a loved one. You're not the first person who's lost a job.

Don't let worrying about your past mistakes hold you back. God will accept you with all of your flaws. When you understand how great God is in your life, you don't have to keep bringing up your past failures. Failure is a wonderful teacher, and when you make mistakes and you recover from them and you treat them as valuable learning experiences, that's when you grow and gain something meaningful to share. It's OK for you to do better, be better, and want better for your life. If you

---

God will accept you with all of your flaws. . . . If you keep moving on your path, God will change your life over time. God will take all your mistakes and failures and package them for your own good.

---

keep moving on your path, God will change your life over time. God will take all your mistakes and failures and package them for your own good.

Don't let other people's opinion of what you've done in your past or can do in your future hold you back either. I've done a lot of things in my life that I haven't always been proud of. But I recognize that I am the sum total of my past. You can't let anyone hold you to your past. You know what you used to do. You know where you used to be. When God forgives your mistakes, you don't have any reason in the world to let someone's opinion of who you used to be stop you from getting where you are trying to go.

Move forward. When the relationship is over, what are you going to do? Are you going to stay there and wonder why it ended? If you do that, you'll be preventing a new relationship from happening, because you've buried yourself in the old one. Sometimes the best deal is to let someone else take that "used car" off your hands—the one that's broken, don't work right, stalls out, runs hot, got no brakes, sputters, has cracked tail lights and a blown engine! Maybe it wasn't the right relationship for you. You have to keep moving forward to the next one—but during that time, work on yourself, enjoy being single for a minute, do the things you couldn't do before in your relationship. Enjoy your time alone. Work on yourself. Determine what you really want in a partner. This "lesson period" is perfect for figuring it out. And the lesson is that if one man wanted you, I can promise you that two more have wanted you along the way, too.

Behind every disappointment there is a purpose, a message. Flunking out of Kent State taught me a valuable lesson. It showed me that I had no vision when I went to college. When you jump with a vision of who you are, why you are here, and where you want to go, that's when you jump with purpose.

Remember that God's plan is always greater than your plan for yourself.

I met a woman on campus at Kent State named Ida Washington. She thought I was funny, and she would always say to me, "Steve, you missed your calling. You should be on TV." She was the first person to ever speak those words into my life other than me. They had a more profound effect on me than she'll ever know. If I'd gone to Kent only to hear Ida say those words to me, then my time there was truly invaluable, even without a degree.

You cannot expect to get everything you want, just the way you want it. It took leaving college for me to find my path. Sometimes God allows us to go through an experience to get a different lesson from the one we expected.

On your journey, pursue your passion in such a way that you are open to other opportunities. The most important lessons can be learned only through your experiences as you go through life's ups and downs, hills and valleys—the successes and the failures. Use the experiences to uncover the gift that God put inside you, and be on a mission to unlock the doors that will lead to your success, one failure at a time. The road to success is always under construction; there will be detours, roadblocks, bumps, and dead ends. But when life takes you off course, open your eyes to the possibilities of the new road ahead of you. Try not to be so focused on only one path or one goal. It's normal to be frustrated or disappointed when you face adversity, but you never know if not taking a road has led you away from making a huge mistake, or off the wrong path. God puts those detours in your way so you can get to the road that you are supposed to be on.

A while after I got laid off from Ford, I applied for a job as a field agent for Allstate. I'd never been through such an extensive interview process. I went on six different interviews for that position. Every time, I would suit up and bring my A game for the interview. When I came back the sixth time, the HR manager told me, "Steve, you're just not the kind of guy we want at Allstate." I could have been disappointed or frustrated or felt like I'd wasted my time. But I looked at that closed door and kept walking down the hallway to my next interview as an insurance agent at another company, and I got that job. I quit in less than a year. Of course, I couldn't have known then that my rejection from All-state and my quitting my job at another company would eventually lead me to unlocking my gift as a comedian. But being open to that detour and being willing to try another door created the opportunity for me to be redirected to the path that has led me to where I am today.

God never promised you that life would be a smooth journey from one place to another. The low points in your life are as necessary for you as the high points. The mistake that too many people make is allowing those tough times to keep them in one place.

Once you get to a roadblock and face adversity, you think, "Hey, God, I don't want that anymore. I can't do this." Nobody wants to willingly face adversity or to struggle in life. But in order to develop and grow, and ultimately to be able to jump to the next level, you have to be able to face adversity along the way and move past it.

Have you ever seen a little kid get on the monkey bars? The monkey bars are no fun if you stay on one bar. The thing about the monkey bars is you've got to let go of the bar you're on to get to the next one. You have to put one hand up, let go, put your other hand up, let go. That is the only way monkey bars are fun. If you are hanging on to one bar and not trying to get to the next, not only are you not having any fun, but you also aren't going to get to the other side. It's the same with adversity. You've got to focus on the other side, and that helps you get through it. You have to put one hand over the other and keep going.

You don't have to know how God will bring you to where you should be. You just need to have faith. I trust and know that I'm not doing this thing by myself. I know that my blessings aren't because I'm perfect and have never made any mistakes, or that I've never failed. I've failed more times than I've succeeded. I know that it's God's grace that has allowed me to keep moving forward in my life.

I am always open to God's plan for me. I am always ready to jump to the next level, because my life has taught me that God's plan for me will always be greater than I can imagine. That's the beauty of jumping. You never know where you will land. Even if you fail, you can still end up with opportunities or skills or connections that you wouldn't possess if you hadn't tried. This road that I'm traveling now has given me access to opportunities that I didn't even know were possible. The more time you spend thinking about failures, or things that didn't work out, places that you didn't go, connections that you missed, or ones who got away, the less time you have to enjoy exactly where you are right now, and to consider where you can go next.

One of the last jobs I had at Ford was working in the foundry where they make engine blocks. Engine blocks start with scrap metal. The scrap metal is put into a furnace and then melted down. The liquid metal is then poured into a mold. When the liquid is poured in, it's a very hot liquid. Then a crane comes along and pulls the hot liquid out of the frame, dips it, cools it, and refinishes it. Then it goes on a conveyor belt. My job was to hit it with a sledgehammer to make sure that any loose metal fell away. Now, you have an engine block. It is a part of the engine that drives a car. But you have to realize that engine block started from scraps, from barely nothing.

God can take the scraps of your life, turn them into your engine of determination to succeed, and help you soar higher than you have ever been before. You don't have to wait to be perfect to jump. Nobody's perfect. I'm certainly not. The richest, most successful, most well known people aren't perfect. They did the best with what they had and they never quit. That's how they got to where they are now. You don't have to wait to have every part of your life together. You can't be so proud that you refuse to let God work with the scraps of your life. You have no idea how He will mold your broken pieces into a perfect vessel. You can't even imagine how He will take your broken heart and put you back together again. You might be a high school dropout, but God can present to you the life experiences that will give you wisdom surpassing that of any person with a PhD.

Jumping to your next level of greatness isn't easy. If it were, you'd see more people leaving dead-end jobs and unhappy marriages, and getting to the business of finding out their gift or going for the job of their dreams. But just because it's difficult doesn't mean that it's impossible. It doesn't mean that you shouldn't try to go beyond what you can see is possible in your life. When you take that first jump, it's going to be challenging. But when you jump, learn to jump again and again. With each jump, you develop the confidence to take a bigger leap of faith. With every leap, you gain the faith to take on the next mountain on your path. The more you jump, the more you will look back and be amazed at how far God has brought you.

2

There Are
No Straight Lines
in Nature

Your dream is everything. It's the biggest part of your life, and in the dream lies your greatest opportunity for success.

Enjoy the journey.

Hope requires you to get out of your bed and make something happen every day.

Jumping is a leap necessary to unlock the gift that God has granted you. If you're not willing to jump to get to the next level, you'll end up settling for an unfulfilling life.

There are many reasons that will motivate you to jump. Maybe you're sick and tired of being sick and tired, and you jump. It could be because you want to be happy in your chosen profession.

If you do not jump, your life simply becomes a routine of getting up and going to work every day. If you're working a job that does not excite you, that's not living; it's simply existing. If your focus stays on where you are right now—being unfulfilled, depressed, not working your dream job, not being in a relationship that sustains you—then your right now becomes your forever.

In 1985 I was just existing. I wanted more from my life than working behind a desk at an insurance agency. I wanted to be on television. I wanted a better life as a whole. I took a leap—I quit my job and put everything on the line. With only a dream and my faith in God, I left everything behind. I went for it.

There should be nothing bigger than your dream. Your dream is everything. It's the biggest part of your life. It's the vision and ambition that God placed in your imagination that won't let you sleep at night until you act on it. It's the thing that wakes you up and stirs the very pit of your soul. It is the vision for your life that is approved by God. Your dream is most important to make manifest, because each and every one of us is a child of God. He doesn't want His children to do without. The dream that He put in your imagination is part of His grand plan for taking care of all His children. For instance, your dream may be to start a high-end arts program that travels throughout city schools, exposing kids to various fields, such as culinary arts, floral arranging, filmmaking, writing, sculpting, and the like. One of the children could be inspired and go on to become a great artist, beautifying the world with his work. We're all connected. Our dreams influence and affect the dreams of others. Your dreams are not just for you. They are for the world's benefit. Go after your dream with a passion!

I brought my dream together with my gift—and I jumped. I cannot stress enough that God has given each and every one of us a gift. In your gift lies your greatest opportunity for success. How do you determine what your gift is? Very simply: Your gift is the thing that you do the absolute best with the least amount of effort. That's your gift.

> God has given each and every one of us a gift. In your gift lies your greatest opportunity for success.

As I said in *Act Like a Success, Think Like a Success*, I thought my gift was the ability to make people laugh. However, I have come to learn that my gift is sharing information effectively by using humor. Are you gifted with numbers? When you arrive at a party, are you instinctively the kind of person who needs to know everyone in the room? Could you see yourself being someone who attends parties and makes sure the right introductions are made? Are you gifted with the camera? Do you enjoy refurbishing old houses? Are you gifted at molding glass?

When I took my leap, I believed, as the Scripture promises, that His blessings would overcome me and chase me down, and that I would receive all the things I had asked for and had hoped for. These sentiments are so engrained in my psyche that when things do not go the way I had planned, I know there must be something better for me. And it's those expectations—those hopes—that allow something better for me to come into place. You have got to take the gift that's packed away on your back, in your backpack, and you have to jump off the cliff and pull the cord. Your gift will open up and let you soar.

Whenever I dare to hope, I know that God's blessings will overtake me. The kind of hope I am talking about is when you realize that you are creating your life with God. The kind of hope I'm talking about is mapping a plan for what you want and how you plan to achieve it. The kind of hope I am talking about requires you to get out of your bed and make something happen in your life *every day*. The kind of hope I am talking about will motivate you to find that thing you were created on earth to do. I know it's hard to see God's abundance when you have bills coming at you so fast you don't know how you will keep up. Trust me, I've been there and back. I've lost everything I've owned—*twice*. But it costs you nothing to hope. It costs you nothing to dream again. It costs you nothing to open your heart and love again. It costs you nothing to believe that that little bit of hope in your heart can create a life far beyond your dreams.

I don't worry when my hope doesn't work out the way that I planned. It puts me in a position to try something new. My only job is to keep getting up and allow my hope to propel my life forward. Every morning that I am blessed to see another day, it is yet another chance I have to dream again. It is an opportunity for me to see how I can do it better. It is another opportunity to jump toward the life that God has planned for me. There's no such thing as a hollow hope. I've lived through enough to know that God's plans for me will always be better than anything I could ever dream of.

My hope and faith enabled me to quit my steady insurance job and create two hundred business cards with the title "Comedian." I jumped from merely existing to trying to make something happen in my life. I climbed into my old car and hit the road. All I knew was that I could make people laugh. So I started there. That was my plan. I had never even heard of a comedy club. But that didn't stop me from trying stand-up for the first time.

I was a twenty-seven-year-old traveling from gig to gig in cities all over the country. My first month as a comedian I made $125. The next month I made $75. As the months wore on, sometimes I pulled in less than $50. The little money I did make, I would send to my wife to help take care of my daughters.

My first year as a comedian, I made less than $4,000. My relationship with my family began to fall apart. I was on my own. It was hard for me to respect myself as a man when I didn't know if I would be guaranteed a paycheck. But jumping from a dead-end job as an insurance agent wasn't just about taking a blind risk; it was about making a leap necessary for me to unlock the gift that God had planted in my imagination.

Bishop T. D. Jakes told me that "to get to the next level you have to break through a glass ceiling. But when you break through glass there's going to be bloodshed." You sometimes have to give up what you love the most to do what you do best. If you're not willing to work hard and to sacrifice, if you're not willing to jump to get to the next level, you'll end up settling for an unfulfilling life.

That was not me. I had my father's work ethic and my mother's faith. I believed they were an unbeatable combination to sustain me. I never quit; I never gave up. I sat there in my car night after night. I accepted the fact that I had nowhere to go. I resigned myself to the fact that I didn't have a bathroom to wash up in.

During those dark days, I'd hear a voice in my head say, "If you keep going, I'm going to take you places you've never been." What kept me going was my faith that God would not give me more than I could handle, and the hope that I might one day be on television—my faith that He would catch me when I jumped.

Sure, sometimes you can plan a jump. You can see it coming and you're ready to make the jump. But sometimes a jump is not a jump; it's a push. You can be pushed, and the ground under your feet will give way. You'll stumble, and the next thing you know you are off the cliff. You move to the next level because a situation has forced you to move. Maybe you want to open a business but you think, "Not now, not now, not now," and you put it off. Then you go in to work and find out the company is closing. Now you are off the cliff, ready or not! Maybe you are at work thinking, "I'm going to get a new job, I'm gonna do it." Then the boss comes in and says something crazy to you and you respond back, and then your boss yells at you and you snap back. The next thing you know, you're fired. You're off the cliff, ready or not. When my daughter got married, she got pregnant on her honeymoon. They weren't really talking about having a family, but she got pregnant right away. Guess what? Little Ben is here! The little girl I used to hold in my arms, that little girl is holding her own baby in her arms. Ready or not, you're off that cliff.

While I was living out of my car, when the nights were cold in the winter or hot in the summer, it would have been easy for me to get discouraged. But, being the optimistic person that I am, I looked for affirmation in everything around me that I was doing what I had to do. For instance, as I drove around God's beautiful country from show to show, I noticed that there are no straight lines in nature. This world is beautiful because of the curves of its mountain peaks, its valleys, its crevices, its waterfalls, its lakes, rivers, and rambling brooks. They are beautiful in all their various shapes and forms.

I recognized that the same beauty is found in life. You'll go through high points and you'll go through low points. You'll have to cross mountains and go through valleys. You'll pass lakes and running streams. And, as in nature, those crevices, cracks, and unexpected alignments that give nature its beauty and character are the same crevices, cracks, and unexpected alignments that give you your beauty and character. Don't be so rigid and structured that you lose the fluidity of life, the curves and the bends of life, the shape of life.

There are no straight lines in nature, and there are no straight lines in life. I don't know why we'd expect life to not have twists and turns, ups and downs. It's part of what makes life living. It's part of what makes us the people we are when we get through it. Just as you do at the end of a beautiful walk in nature, when you get to your destination in life, you have a wonderful set of experiences that you've gained and learned from. And you have a wonderful story to tell anybody on the road behind you.

The most beautiful things in the world are not an exact, perfect shape. The sun is beautiful, but what's the exact shape of the sun? The moon is imperfect, it has craters, but it's one of the most beautiful things I've ever seen. Lakes are imperfect, but lakes are some of the most beautiful places on earth. Look at the shoreline of an ocean; it's always flowing and moving—that's what gives it beauty. We have to flow and keep moving like water. Do not be so rigid that you lose sight of how life moves. If you can't flow, then you become stuck where you are. You may never be uncomfortable, but you'll never grow or see what wonderful plan God has for you. It's critical to participate in life, to invest in it if you want something extraordinary back.

Hoping is an investment. While I was on the road, there were moments when I felt that my parachute would never open. It was times like those when I used my imagination to hope for a bigger life. I needed to see beyond my then and there. I had to envision what God had planned for me. To entertain myself in the car, I would let my imagination run wild. I would see beautiful homes and imagine I lived in them with my family. I would see luxury cars and imagine that my career would take me to a place where I might be able to have such a car. Whether I wanted that specific model and make or not didn't matter. It was the hope of better things that kept me going.

Albert Einstein said, "Imagination is everything." It's the preview to life's coming attractions! While I was living in my car, my imagination *was* everything. I imagined the amazing gigs I would get. I imagined the big audiences laughing at my jokes. I imagined achieving my dream. Live the life you want in your imagination, and it can be made real. Someone imagined the cell phone, and that's why we're all attached to our phones right now. The Wright brothers imagined flying in an airplane, and that started the whole field of aviation. Think about where you live: You had a realtor walk you through your home or your apartment, and you imagined your furniture there before you were even approved to sign the lease or get your mortgage. The car you drive, you imagined yourself driving it off the lot before you finished the paperwork, before you even went down to the dealership. If your imagination can open the door to the home you live in and the car you drive, why do you think that you can't use your imagination to open your business or send your kids to the school of their dreams? Start imagining the life you want to live.

Imagining my life to come helped keep my spirits up when I was living in my car, especially since my pay usually wasn't enough to get gas and buy myself dinner. In general, life on the road was uncomfortable at times. When I was lucky, the venue would pay for me to stay in a hotel where they provided a complimentary continental breakfast. Staying someplace like the Sheraton was a joy to me. Man, I had a hotel room! Having my own bathroom for a night was unbelievable. I would take four showers in a day because, damn, they had running water. On some occasions, I would just sit on the toilet. Until you are homeless, you don't even know what a luxury it is to sit on a toilet for as long as you want—even if you don't have to go!

When I didn't have the rare room, I slept in my car with the front seat reclined all the way back. I washed up in gas station restrooms or snuck into hotels and used the bathrooms. There was a night when I hid out in a bathroom stall until the early hours of the morning so no one would see me. There were days that I survived on bologna sandwiches.

On the occasions when I was absolutely starving, I would go into a grocery store and get a whole cart full of food that I couldn't afford. I'd make a sandwich out of the bread and ham I'd gotten, and I would eat the sandwich as I walked around the store. I would make sandwiches out of a whole pack of ham and eat them while I walked around the store because I was so hungry. There weren't many days like those, but there were enough to make me appreciate the little bit I had. I'm not suggesting anyone go out and do this today, 'cause that's stealing and it could get ugly. God covered me, and I'm thanking God for the covering He gives us when we're going through our rough spots.

I did whatever I had to do. But I believed in God's plan for me. I always kept my vision in front of me. I accepted any gig that I could get no matter where it was. Nobody hired me because I had a name or because they knew me. I was hired because I was willing to drive all over the country, show up, and do the gig. I never turned down one single gig. I didn't care how far it was. I appreciated all those gigs, and I always gave the best performance that I could. I showed up; I was investing in my hope and dreams.

As I drove around from gig to gig, for inspiration I would hum the theme song from *The Tonight Show Starring Johnny Carson*. Back when I was on the road in the late 1980s, I was told that one out of every two thousand comedians could make it to *The Tonight Show*. If Johnny called you over to the couch, your career was made. At this point, I was so far from Hollywood and *The Tonight Show* that it wasn't even funny. But I hoped my investment would get me somewhere. So whether it was Flint, Michigan, or Fort Lauderdale, Florida, I would start up my car, get down the road, and hum *The Tonight Show*'s opening bars, "*Dun, dun, dun dun duh. Dada dada dada.*"

In crafting your dream, do not let statistics get in the way. Statistics are for losers who need to justify why they never got into the game of their life. I did not care that one out of every two thousand comedians makes it on to *The Tonight Show*. When I heard that, I just figured that they weren't talking to me. My attitude was, "Man, wait till they get a load of me! I can't wait for Johnny Carson to see my tape!" (Johnny Carson never saw my tape. I never made it to his couch. I doubt he even knew I existed. And, maybe it's a good thing he didn't see my tape back then—they're even hard for me to watch!)

Just that little thing of humming the *Tonight Show* theme song helped me turn my hope into faith. Right now, you might not have the faith, and that's OK. Eventually your hope will help you build the faith you need to go to the next level. In the beginning of my career, I didn't have the faith that I would be on television. I just hoped that I would one day.

Being who I am, I maintained my sense of humor on the road, because it is important to enjoy your journey—speed bumps, potholes, and all. I had to laugh at eating bologna sandwiches for a whole week. I found the humor in waking up and not knowing where I was. I often couldn't afford to buy a newspaper, but sometimes I would search for one to find out what city I was in. That to me was funny, to wake up and not know what city I was in. I found the humor in sitting there in my car wondering where I was and what I could see that would help me figure it out.

One morning I woke up in Florida after pulling over on the side of the road in the middle of the night to sleep. I had parked against a barbed wire fence. It was hot, so I'd rolled down the windows. When I woke up from my deep sleep, I saw this big pink thing wiggling through the passenger's side window. I thought it was a large snake. In a hurry I started climbing out the driver's-side window. Running for my life, I crawled out so fast that I fell on the ground. This car that was coming up the road stopped and the driver asked if I was okay, since I was laid out on the ground. I was about to say a snake was in my car when I saw the cow. Behind a fence, a cow had leaned over and stuck his tongue in my car window. Now, tell me there's no humor in that!

Another time, I was on my way to El Paso, Texas. I pulled up to a lake to go to sleep for the night. I was about five or six feet from the lake. It was beautiful. I ate a bologna sandwich then fell asleep. When I woke up, I was in water up to my bumper and it had just started seeping into the car. I opened my eyes from sleep and saw that my feet were wet. I panicked. I opened the door and more water came in. My heart was pounding. I'm thinking, "Did my car slide into the middle of the lake?" I'm standing there and this guy drives up, sees me and my car in the water, and says, "You know at the levee they raise the water level on the lake sometimes at night." I'm standing there looking at my car almost submerged in water. I laughed so hard. I had to get a tow truck because the car wouldn't start and I couldn't get it out. Most people wouldn't find that funny, but it was funny to me. I always tried to find humor even in those low moments.

Although I was not beating myself up for being homeless, I was not advertising it either. In other words, I did not believe that most of the people I came across on the circuit knew that I was living out of my car. I did not make a big deal of my situation. I remained positive and open to new experiences though. And I think my attitude brought good people into my life.

There was a guy I knew in Augusta, Georgia, when I used to play at the Comedy House Theater there. His name was Charlie Williams, and he had an auto glass shop. I had a cooler in the back of my car. I kept it filled with ice. It was my refrigerator. I kept bologna, bread, cheese, and mustard in there. I would get a roll of bologna—the kind with the red tape all around it, which would last for a long time. A cooler was one of the best items a homeless man could have!

One day, Charlie was cooking in his shop. He was making this stuff called Georgia hash in a big pot. Charlie gave me a big Tupperware full of hash. It was the most delicious meal. Best thing I ever ate. He loaded me up. Every time I came through Augusta, he would fill my cooler up with food. I think he knew that something was wrong. But he never asked. He just helped me. He is my friend to this day! It is people like Charlie who kept me going during those homeless years. I'll never forget what he did for me.

While I was living in my car, I certainly did not feel successful. When you're homeless there's not a lot of positivity in that, but I would find little things that I could hang my hope on. Through all my mistakes, I always hoped that one day I'd get on television. When I flunked out of college, I hoped that one day I'd get on television. When I was getting a divorce, I was hoping I'd get on television. There was never a moment when I said, "If I don't get on television, what am I gonna do?" I was already doing it. The alternative to going for my dream—to sacrificing, to jumping—was *not going* for it. That simply was not an option for me.

Faith kept me on course. Faith is the substance of things hoped for. It's not faith at first. Faith is built around the substance of things *hoped* for. I just *hoped* I'd get on television; I didn't have *faith* I was going to get there—I was just hoping. Then, as opportunities got closer, my hope turned into faith.

The process that gets you on the road to hope will lead you on a path of faith. Faith is believing in your dream. But faith without works is a death sentence for your hopes and dreams. The scripture in James 2:14 says, "Faith without works is dead. What does it profit,

"Faith without works is dead. What does it profit, my brethren, if someone says he has faith but does not have works? Can faith save him?"
—JAMES 2:14

my brethren, if someone says he has faith but does not have works? Can faith save him?"

In other words, your dreams aren't free. You can dream all day long, but if you don't put in the work, your dreams will never become a reality. You can dream all you want, but if you are not willing to put in the work, you're dreaming in vain. The only way you'll know if your dream is worth pursuing is if you get up and do the work. Your dreams are attainable; God is just waiting for you to do your part. You have to be committed to dedicating your life to something bigger than yourself, pass the tests that will come along the way, and stay the course through the end. If you quit, there's no way you will know what God has in store for you.

I didn't know I could be a comedian when I quit my job as an insurance agent. I started out with a faith in my gift, and I imagined where it might take me. As I said, I expected and believed that His blessings would overcome me and chase me down. I believed that I would receive all the things that I asked for. I expect the good. I have faith that what I imagine will manifest in my life. You can do the same.

Keep putting one foot in front of the other, even if you don't know the way. It's not your job to know the way; it's just your job to believe. You can't be so focused about trying to figure out every single part of the plan. There's no scripture in the Bible that says you must have your life completely figured out. All you have to do is ask and believe.

The life that God has planned for you, the one that He has specially designed for you, is deeply rooted in your imagination. He has to help you with the jump because in order to get to what you imagine—those far-out thoughts you have of one day being famous, or one day owning your own company, or one day being able to provide for your children's children, or one day creating a legacy for yourself—those dreams are huge. But they are not unattainable. They require an unerring faith and a willingness not only to imagine the life you want to live but also to be willing to work toward it—to jump.

In order to soar to that next level of your life, you have to be willing to be cut by the rocks of life. Those cuts are necessary. When I was homeless, I knew I was paying my dues for my dream. We all have to do that.

God is a trainer. Your cuts or dues will give you the push-through factor. Those cuts and bruises from your jump will make you come with it when you can't come with it anymore. You can get cut so many different ways. It could be someone talking about you on your job. It could be someone accusing you of something that you didn't do. It could be someone sharing information about you that isn't true. Know that those cuts allow you to build your character. You have to trust that God is making you stronger for your next jump.

And He was doing that in my life. God is always working on making things happen for you. Even in your darkest moment, you have to believe this. I know how dark it can get. It was a Thursday; I was on the interstate in Pensacola, Florida, when I was about to give up. I only had a small amount of money and was fixing to go home and ask my father if I could stay in the attic for a little while until I could get on my feet, then I would move out. I got on the phone and called my answering machine, which was located at my mama's house in the attic. They had given me a phone line. I called up there to the house. Voicemail said, "This is Chuck Sutton from *Showtime at the Apollo*. I just saw a tape on you and it was hysterical. We have an opening for Sunday night on the late show. If you can be here, call me back and I'll hold the spot for you." *Beep.*

"Wow! A television appearance!"

I had to sit down and think about it. I had $35 in my pocket. Not enough money to get a plane ticket to New York. And television doesn't pay immediately, like the comedy clubs normally do. Television mails you your money later. I couldn't believe that I was so close to realizing my dream and I didn't have a way to get there. I just sat trying to figure it out. I thought about calling my daddy to see if I could just come to the house. I had enough money to fill up my tank, because back then gas was like a dollar a gallon. I knew I could make it if I didn't eat anything. I got into the car and drove a little bit, then I decided to call my answering machine again. I was thinking that maybe Chuck Sutton didn't say this Sunday. I punched in my code. I listened to the message again. Dang, it was *this* Sunday—two days away. I got ready to hang up the pay phone when I heard "You have another message." I pressed 1. *Beep.* "Steve Harvey, this is Tom Sobel from the Comedy Caravan. I don't know where you are, buddy, but if you're anywhere near Jacksonville, Florida, Friday night, I got a gig for you to be a feature act. If you can get there, buddy, I got $150 for you. Call me back."

"Hey, Tom, it's Steve."

"Hey, Steve, can you make it?"

"I'm about three hours away. I'll be there man."

When I arrived, Tom gave me a room. I walked on-stage and I killed it. I mean, killed it! The dude gave me the $150 as he said, "The regular guy is supposed to be back, but I like you better. I'll give you another $250 if you stay tomorrow night."

"I'm your man!" He gave me the money. I stayed Saturday night. I got up early Sunday morning, packed all my stuff, and drove to the airport. Eastern Airlines was in business then. They had a special round-trip fare, Jacksonville to New York for $99. *Bam!* I bought the ticket. I landed in New York by eleven a.m. But, I didn't go on at the Apollo until eleven p.m.

I didn't have anywhere to go and went straight to the theater. I was at the front entrance ringing the door-bell. This was Harlem; the cleaning man or somebody comes to the door looking at me sideways. "Man, what you doing?"

"I'm performing tonight."

He didn't seem impressed. "You can't come through this front door. All the acts go to the back."

Keep in mind, everything I had in this world I had in my hands. I couldn't leave my stuff in my car, which was parked in Florida, because if somebody broke into it I would not have had any more clothes. I had all my stuff in two large bags and they were heavy. I walked along 125th Street, up Frederick Douglass and all the way around to the back. A security guard who had just gotten there said, "Hey, man, what you want?"

"I'm performing tonight."

"Man, you way too early. We don't open these doors until five."

"Whoa," I said. "Can I just wait right here?"

"Man, why don't you go back to your house or something?"

"I don't live here, man. I caught a plane here."

"Say you ain't from here?"

"Naw, man."

"Why don't you go over to one of your partners' house."

"I don't know nobody up here. Just look, man, if you let me in and tell me where to sit, I'll sit right there. I won't move."

"Comedians on the sixth floor," he replied.

There are no elevators in the Apollo. I dragged my bags up to the sixth floor. I went in and I sat down. By this time it was around twelve thirty or something like that. I was just sitting there hungry. Thirsty. I got some drinking water out of this fountain in the hallway. I didn't go get any food because I couldn't risk leaving my stuff in there. Around five o'clock some other comedians started coming in. I met Dwayne Johnson, Cedric The Entertainer, and Jamie Foxx. We shook hands and introduced ourselves. I had heard of Jamie on the circuit, but we had never met. Finally, they started taping the show. Jamie was on the second show. I was on the fourth. Jamie got booed. They booed him bad. It was wicked. Jamie put the jokes aside and started singing. And he got the audience back for a short while. Then he went back to his jokes and they booed him off the stage. Afterward, Jamie was sitting on the steps. I was walking by to go perform. "Man, what's up? You alright?" I said.

"I got booed. It's never happened to me. It's rough out there."

His words made me more scared. It was the Apollo. I had heard about it. But, I was prepared. I went out onstage and did my famous Mike Tyson joke and ended the night with a standing ovation. My television career was born.

T. D. Jakes says, "I would hate to die and never do the thing I was born to do." Know that this life that you dream about can be yours. That thing that stirs in you, that thing you just can't shake every time you start a career only to find it's just not sitting right—what is that? It's the seed that God put inside you at birth that's been waiting to grow. But it needs nurturing and watering.

For me, success meant doing the thing I was born to do. It was finding my gift. Success should never be exclusively about money. I know a lot of rich people who are miserable and eventually become sick in body and spirit. They would give back every dollar to be healthy. The key to success is to make the most out of life with something you already have. Find what gives you pleasure. Define what success means to you and create a plan for achieving it. When I talk about success, it doesn't necessarily mean money. Your success could be found by expanding your family. It could be found in developing a closer relationship with God. It could mean finding an exceptional spouse. It does not have to mean abruptly quitting your job as I did.

Every successful person in this world has jumped. If you want to nurture that seed inside you, if you want to use your gift, if you want to find the success that is specific to you, you have to jump. If you're waking up every day thinking there has to be more to your life than there is, then believe that there is, but to get that life you have to jump.

The only difference between successful people and others is how seriously and actively they believe in their dreams. Those crazy thoughts and far-out ideas you have of one day being famous, one day being rich, one day owning a summer home, one day being able to provide for your children's children, one day creating a legacy for yourself, those dreams of being the best in your class, running or owning a company one day—see them and hang on to them. Believe in whatever you can imagine. Becoming a writer, having your own trucking company, opening your own salon—whatever it is—that thing you keep imagining can be real. But in order to get what you imagine, to make those dreams real, you have to jump. Making what you imagine requires a jump.

The great things in life aren't nearby, they aren't easy to find, and when you do find them, they aren't easy to get. Diamonds aren't lying around on the ground. Pearls aren't sitting there on the grass waiting for you. Diamonds are found deep in the earth. Pearls are at the bottom of the sea. If you want something more in life, life is going to require more from you. You cannot get it without a massive and sustained effort. You can't find oil without digging miles into the ground, without hard, sustained work. Now, there aren't any guarantees that you will get it, certainly not right away. But I can guarantee that you won't get it if you don't try, if you don't jump. True success is never free; you have to do some work. But imagine if you try and you succeed. Trust me, it will be worth it.

3

If You're Going Through Hell, Keep Going

Embracing adversity is the key to learning who you are under pressure. It builds confidence, which will enable you to reach higher toward your abundant life.

A moment of crisis will show you exactly who you are, and that is your moment to rise above it all.

Life is a series of lessons learned and obstacles overcome.

Successful people know that making decisions often comes with hard choices.

There is absolutely nothing in your life that God hasn't already pulled you though or isn't currently pulling you through.

When you get into trouble, when you find yourself down in a hole, you will not have

to seek out your real true friends. They will
come down and get in that hole with you.

S everal years ago, I joined a new talent management company. It also represented the Miss Universe pageant. With the idea of putting his clients together, my agent asked me if I would host the pageant. I was excited. I considered hosting the Miss Universe pageant, the prospect of facing an audience of a billion—the audience in the theater and the audience watching live on television around the world—to be the pinnacle achievement of my career of many years.

There were three days of rehearsals leading up to the pageant to ensure that we were all well prepared. I was there for every technical rehearsal, which means checking lighting and sound. I was there for every table read, in which we would read the script of the entire show—a run-through. I was at the AXIS, the location of the pageant, at six thirty a.m. on the day of the show for the full-dress rehearsal with all eighty of the contestants.

Leading up to the night of the pageant, I had a chance to connect with many of the women. Ariadna Gutiérrez, Miss Colombia, was an animal lover and ran a foundation to assist underprivileged children. By the age of seventeen, she was working as a model to put herself through college, where she was studying advertising. Pia Wurtzbach, Miss Philippines, was from a single-parent home. She broke into modeling and acting at age eleven to provide for her mother and sister. She had entered the Miss Philippines pageant three times. She won on her third try, to receive the honor of competing for the Miss Universe crown. Growing up, she had spent many hours, days, weeks, and years practicing for the pageant in her room. It had been several decades since a Miss Philippines had been crowned Miss Universe, and she was determined to bring the honor to her homeland again.

Talking to and engaging with these women, I came to understand just how important the pageant was to them. For these talented young ladies, the Miss Universe competition wasn't just about a earning title or winning a crown, it was about bringing honor to their families and countries. They were competing for the distinction of being a global ambassador for their nation. "The world stops in the Philippines when it's Miss Universe time," said Pia. "It's like a Manny Pacquiao boxing match. Everybody is inside watching and waiting for that special moment." The crown was something that these young women had hoped and trained for since they were little girls. The title of Miss Universe was a dream for them in the same way that being able to host the pageant was for me.

During rehearsals, I also got to know a lot of the backstage crew. I'll never forget, Lou, a beautiful older sister who ran all the rehearsals. Lou was a sharp, exacting choreographer who showed the contestants how to walk and where to stand during the show. She was demanding and knowledgeable. She instructed them tirelessly in what they needed to know for the pageant. I observed the women working hard, for hours, during every practice as Lou ran them through walks and positions. She would say, "You're not standing right. Walk with poise. Hold your head up. Strike the pose! Give it to the people. Watch your posture!"

I typically joked with everyone, to keep the atmosphere light. But I also did it to help the contestants relax and enjoy the experience. They appreciated my humor. They told me later that it helped take the edge off their nervousness.

Each day, we practiced the final walk with a first runner-up and a winner. I'd say, "The first runner-up is . . ." and, "The new Miss Universe 2015 is . . . Lou!" I used Lou's name during rehearsal because we didn't want to jinx any of the contestants.

Finally, it was the big night, the night of the pageant. I walked onstage in my white tuxedo jacket and bow tie. The crowd erupted in applause in anticipation of the night's contest. The atmosphere was electric. We were all thrilled to be a part of the excitement. Members of the audience were waving flags representing their countries. We began with the opening promenade and presentation of the contestants, followed by the swimsuit competition, the ball gowns, and the talent display, and closed with the question and answer.

Then we arrived at the moment everyone had been waiting for. There were three women positioned at the front of the stage. They were Miss USA, Miss Colombia, and Miss Philippines—our finalists. I was given the card with the names for the first runner-up, the winner, and the second runner-up. In all the rehearsals, I'd been given only two names. I held the card to my chest with my thumb covering the words *second runner-up*, which was printed on the card. I announced Miss USA as the first runner-up.

The audience applauded. Miss Colombia and Miss Philippines were now front and center. The remaining seventy-eight contestants, all lined up, were standing several feet behind them. Miss Colombia and Miss Philippines were holding hands, surely saying a prayer.

They looked radiant, Miss Philippines in her royal blue gown and Miss Colombia in a bronze-colored sparkly number. The spotlight was on the two women. Miss Colombia's name was on the next card.

I read the teleprompter the same as I had over the past three days: "And the new Miss Universe 2015 is"—in my ear I heard, *Hold . . . hold . . . hold . . . NOW READ!*—"Miss Colombia!" I exited the stage as the place went crazy. The audience was screaming with delirium. Miss Colombia put her hands over her eyes in disbelief before reaching for Miss Philippines and hugging her. The lights came up. The yellow bulbs looked like a golden waterfall cascading behind the women. The Miss Universe sash was placed around Miss Colombia. Tears rolled down her face. There was pandemonium in the crowd. Miss Colombia was given flowers and a Colombian flag. She was beaming at the audience as she waved her country's flag. The crowd screamed their love to her. At the same time, her cousin, a former Miss Colombia, entered the stage with the crown in her hand. They kissed on the cheek and hugged each other. Paulina Vega crowned Ariadna Gutiérrez Miss Universe. The light show morphed into a spectacular silver tunnel-like visual. The audience was jumping up and down waving flags. Ariadna was alternating between blowing kisses to them, waving, placing her hand over her heart, pumping her fist, and wiping her tears. There was a group of fans from Colombia holding up signs and going wild in the front row.

Then, as I stood backstage, I heard in my earpiece, "That's the wrong name!" I looked at the card I was holding in my hand with the names of the runners-up and the winner. I saw that the name of the winner was written in the bottom right of the card and not in the middle. This was not the format that I expected or what we'd rehearsed.

Backstage there was chaos. I heard in the earpiece, "We have to fix this." Onstage the applause remained thunderous. Miss Colombia was still crying and the audience was clapping.

At the top of the night of the pageant, one of the backstage managers who had previously worked at another pageant said, "The final walk should actually be second runner-up, first runner-up, and then the winner." No one relayed that information to me or to the person feeding the teleprompter. I stood there stunned. I was confused and disappointed that I had said the wrong name. How could this have happened?

In the midst of this, I heard my father saying, "Be a man. Stand up. Put your hands on your lower back. Brace yourself. Square your chin. Stick out your chest and handle it." I heard my mother echoing, "You have to do the right thing by people, even if it hurts you." My parents taught me how to be a man in the face of adversity. In those three minutes, I wasn't a television host. In that moment, I was my mother and father's son. I knew that the right thing to do was to fix the mistake immediately and give Miss Philippines her rightful moment on air to be crowned as Miss Universe.

In that moment, I had a decision to make, and it would not be an easy one. Yes, I had the option of staying backstage and letting the events unfold without doing anything. I did not have to shoulder the responsibility in front of the world for this mistake. But that's not how my parents raised me. My only choice was to rectify the situation. I have a plaque on my desk that reads IF YOU'RE GOING THROUGH HELL, KEEP GOING. I would not stop. I had to move forward. This moment of adversity forced me to lead with my character. I had to jump.

The pageant was important to the contestants. They'd worked most of their lives to stand on that stage and represent their country and their family. Winning Miss Universe could change the life of one of these young women forever. I couldn't deny the rightful winner her opportunity to take her walk onstage as Miss Universe.

I also thought about the jobs that would be on the line for that mistake. There was no time for finger-pointing or passing the blame. I'm not in the finger-pointing business. I'm in the ownership business.

I had already paid my dues to be on television. I had a twenty-year track record of successfully hosting shows. But there were people backstage that night who might not easily get another job if they had to shoulder a mistake like this. There were young people on that crew who would have their careers tarnished. I couldn't walk away. It was only sensible for me to be Jesse and Eloise's son and do the right thing.

My decision to walk back on that stage was a result of everything my parents had taught me. I was anchored by the core of who I've always been—the person my parents had taught me to be and my faith in God—when I prepared to jump.

It wasn't about me. God had brought me to this moment, and I had to trust that He'd bring me through it. There were people backstage who wanted to leave everything as it was and then issue a press release the following day. I could not live with that. I felt that Miss Universe should have her moment

God had brought me to this moment, and I had to trust that He'd bring me through it.

in the spotlight. She deserved to be crowned in front of everyone. I had to rectify my mistake right away.

I forced my feet to take me back onstage. And, believe me, it was hard. Miss Colombia's supporters were still yelling, screaming, and waving flags, as she waved back at them. I walked slowly to where she stood. It took a full two minutes for the cheers and music to die down. I started with, "I have to apologize." At this point, Miss Colombia turned around; she was facing the other contestants, who were lined up at the back of the stage. She turned to me when my words registered. She was wiping tears from her eyes and was laughing. I glanced at the card in my hand. It was tougher than I thought to get the words out. The audience's shouts of joy and applause were deafening; I could barely be heard over the noise. I was thinking, "I gotta fix it. I gotta fix this." I had to tell Miss Colombia and the audience and everyone watching all across the world that I had made a mistake, that she was not Miss Universe. The contestants were laughing. They were thinking I was telling some kind of joke, as I'd done in the rehearsals. Finally, as the crowd settled down a little bit, I said slowly and clearly, "The first runner-up is Miss Colombia."

There was a moment of silence, then the crowd started cheering again. There was confusion on Miss

Philippines' face. She whispered something to Miss USA. Pia began to figure out that since Miss Colombia was the first runner-up, then she was Miss Universe. She placed her hand over her heart.

"Miss Universe 2015 is Miss Philippines," I announced.

Miss Philippines walked forward tentatively with her hand now covering her mouth. Once she got closer to Miss Colombia, she slowed her steps even more. It was clear that both women were uncomfortable. The stage lights returned to imitate a golden rain shower. Paulina Vega came back to the stage and stood between the women. She placed her hand on Miss Colombia's back and gently stroked it in consolation.

"Listen folks, let me just take control of this. This is exactly what's on the card. I will take responsibility for this. It was my mistake; it was on the card. A horrible mistake, but the right thing, I can show it to you right here." I held up the card with the names and said, "The first runner-up is Miss Colombia. It is my mistake. . . . Please don't hold it against the ladies."

Pauline Vega removed the crown from Miss Colombia and placed it on Miss Philippines' head.

There was a line of Colombians in the front row who went from cheering to booing. They started screaming, "Liar, liar! It's a fix!" All I could do in that moment was what I was raised to do: I took full responsibility for what happened. I took whatever lashes they had to give me.

When I walked backstage the second time, all hell had broken loose, but a calm had settled over me as I walked to my dressing room. I'd taken responsibility and acted like the man my parents had taught me to be. I had jumped into the midst of the catastrophe and tried to make it right.

A few minutes later, the director entered my dressing room. He said, "Sorry, Steve. Everybody makes mistakes."

I didn't tell him that nobody had told me or the person who was in charge of the teleprompter that there would be three names to announce instead of two, the way we'd practiced in rehearsal. I just listened.

"We are going to hold a press conference, and I don't want you to say anything," he said.

I shook my head. "No, I'm going to the press conference and I'm going to tell them what I did."

"Steve, you don't have to do that."

"Yes, I do. I was raised to be a man and to take responsibility for my actions, even if I don't have to. I won't be a coward or a punk just because it might be difficult or unpleasant."

A moment of crisis showed me exactly who I was, and it will do the same for you. The minute your life falls

> *That moment of crisis isn't happening to you— it's happening for you.*

apart, you can't pretend to be anyone other than who God created you to be. Embracing adversity is the key to learning who you are under pressure. It builds character, which will enable you to reach higher toward your abundant life. That moment of crisis isn't happening to you—it's happening *for* you. This isn't the time for you to crawl in the corner and be a victim. This is your time to learn who you are when times get tough. This is your opportunity to see just how much you've learned from what you've been through previously in your life. Life is a series of lessons learned and obstacles overcome.

When the blame is falling on your shoulders, even when the blame should be spread around, you have to know that there is a reason why you are being singled out. It might be happening to you because the other people in your department can't afford to get suspended for three days. You could be questioning why your child is the one who is always in the principal's office. You might even be facing another round of a health crisis. You have to realize that your moment of adversity is your moment to rise above it all. Don't fight it. Wait on the lesson.

I went to the press conference right after the show. The room was packed. There were at least thirty reporters ready to fire off questions. The room was so crowded that I could barely even see most of them. I envisioned that my purpose for being there was to take as much of the heat as possible. I apologized for what happened. As the reporters yelled questions at me, I answered as thoroughly and as clearly as I could. By the end of the press conference, most of the reporters were responding positively to my answers. They saw that I wasn't throwing around blame. They could see that I was taking full responsibility for the mistake.

But there was a Colombian reporter in the room who was giving it to me. He screamed at me, "How could you do such a thing? How could you make a mistake like that? That's never happened in the history of the pageant! What's your problem? You can't read?"

Some of the other reporters tried to calm him down. They kept telling him, "He said he's sorry." He wouldn't listen. At the end of the conference, most of the reporters put their phones and recorders down and clapped for me.

Even in the middle of that heat, I still felt I had done the right thing. How we handle our mistakes is paramount to our success. My mistake was not an act of failure. It was a valuable lesson gained and learned. Every mistake any of us make—that baby you had out of wedlock, that failed relationship, that job you got fired from, those people who said you weren't going to make it—all those things are valuable lessons for your journey. I recommend that you lean into the lessons. Thomas A. Edison said, "I have not failed. I've just found ten thousand ways that won't work."

I left the press conference depleted and emotionally exhausted. I was relieved that it was time to leave. I overheard my son Wynton say to my bodyguard, "I want to stay with my dad." He could have gotten into another car with the rest of my team, but he stayed right there with me. My youngest son has been with me through so much. It meant everything to have him with me, by my side, in one of my darkest hours. We arrived at what was supposed to be a celebratory dinner with my family and friends, but the mood around the table was somber, reflecting the last few hours after the pageant. I could feel everyone's love and support, though. My wife, Marjorie, held my hand and rubbed my back and neck as she sat next to me at the table. She knew that I was in a world of pain. My children sat opposite us. I could sense that they were proud of me for walking back out onto that stage and taking responsibility. It helped me through some of the pain I felt. I couldn't have gotten through it without their encouragement.

After dinner we went back to the hotel. I finally went to bed at midnight, but I tossed and turned. I couldn't sleep and moved to the sitting area. It was two a.m. Feeling my absence, Marjorie woke up and joined me.

I questioned, "God, how did this happen?"

Marjorie held my hand. "Steve, don't beat yourself up. I know this is tough, but your parents would be so proud of you right now."

Her words reminded me of what was really important. I'd done the right thing. I'd made sure the right Miss Universe was crowned in front of her audience. I'd jumped by shouldering the responsibility. I'd jumped even though I wished I were not in that position. I'd jumped because I had to. I could have taken the easy way out and blamed the pageant, the teleprompter, anybody, anything. Instead, I jumped into an uncomfortable situation with the faith that God would see me through. My family was proud of me, and I knew my parents were proud, too.

The next day my mistake was on every news station, radio program, and social media outlet. I couldn't turn on my computer without a video, meme, or social media post popping up. I was on the front page of papers across the country and around the world. I got personal calls from representatives for Matt Lauer from the *Today* show and Robin Roberts from *Good Morning America*. They reached out and offered to do exclusive interviews with me so I could clear my name. There were producers from other shows who even offered me money for an interview. I turned them all down. I did not feel that moment was about firing back and presenting excuses for the mistake or how it happened. I would not accomplish anything by creating more noise in the media. "Let me have Christmas with my family. Let me wait and see what God tells me," I told them. My job was to sit still and to wait for the lesson and the blessing that God was preparing for me—even though at the time I did not see either.

I know from past experience that it's necessary to be still during times of confusion. When you feel confused, when you do not know what to do, when you are unsure and do not see a clear path to your destination or goal, when you feel swamped and inundated—this is the time to wait on God's peace to come. In that peace you can think clearly. It's difficult to make good decisions when all is swirling around you. You can make smart, informed choices only when your mind is still.

It's normal to have some anxiety after a major jump. It's a place you haven't been before. You need time to adjust. You need space to contemplate options and listen to the voice of God. I needed to sit still to see where He was going to guide me. I had to wait for Him to show me what was next.

Inevitably, when you sit still, somebody is going to recognize what an honorable thing you have done. Anyone in a position of authority will know because they have been there, too. Any successful person knows that most decisions have to come by making hard choices. It's only a matter of time before someone says, "She took the heat, she held her head high, and now a few more people can hold on to their jobs. She did the right thing." Your son or your daughter may not appreciate it now, but they will be able to look back and see that your being hard on them when they decided to be a knucklehead will have an ultimate payoff in their future. They will come to thank you for the lessons.

We are all going to have a moment when it feels like our entire world, whether it's our department, our company, our marriage, or even our relationship with our children, is crumbling around us, and we are forced to shoulder the shame, the blame, and the responsibility for a situation that doesn't belong to us. It's not necessary to waste time wondering why it's happening. If it's in your hands, know that you can handle it. There is absolutely nothing in your life that God hasn't already pulled you through or He isn't currently pulling you through.

Although I was surrounded by my loving family, who nourished and replenished me, I withdrew into myself. This has become my norm when I feel indecisive and have become unsure of what to do. I'll sit and wait to hear God's voice with a plan. I was quiet. I sat listening and thinking. I was waiting for a message, for direction from God. I did not question why this had happened. I was at peace with my response by jumping and atoning for the mistake on the spot. I had replayed the situation over and over in my head and came to the realization that I would not have handled it any differently. I *had* to step out on faith.

The only thing that did not sit right with me was Miss Colombia and Miss Philippines. They were two women thrust into my mistake. I felt horrible and could not stop wondering how they were doing. In my silence, God told me not to do any interviews until I apologized to Miss Colombia. The situation had to be the worst for her because the crown was placed on her head only to be taken off.

The next day, I flew back home to Atlanta. When I got off the plane I discovered that the media storm had gotten even worse. My social media team had written "I'm sorry, Miss Columbia" on Twitter and had misspelled Colombia. So now I had people saying, "You don't even know how to spell Colombia!"

My social media team was panicking. They wanted to respond immediately. I told them, "Don't nobody say nothing to nobody!"

People were having a field day on the Internet. Other entertainers and so-called friends of mine started forwarding and posting memes that were popping up in social media. They'd text, "Hey man, hang in there," followed by a meme mocking the mistake. One was a picture of Oprah. She had her hands thrown in the air proclaiming, "You're Miss Universe and you're Miss Universe. Everybody is Miss Universe!" Another was a picture of Kermit the Frog and the words, "Y'all laughing at Steve Harvey but some of y'all announced the wrong father of your child."

They were trying to joke me through it. I write jokes for a living. I did not need any jokes. I needed prayer. I was hurting in ways my "friends" could not have imagined, because they had never been in the kind of situation I was in.

While I was sitting still, the world was racing. They were eating me alive on social media. My children are always on their computers. They are constantly connecting with people on social media, for me and for my companies. They were devastated to see their father being humiliated all over the Internet. In just forty-eight hours, I had nearly four billion impressions on social media.

On Christmas Eve I tried to pull up an Elmo video for Rose, my granddaughter, and there I was in a meme on social media. My sons tried to make the situation a little lighter by calling me the Social Media King. But at that point I knew that I had to stop watching and reading everything that was posted.

I'm not convinced that people can comprehend their life's lessons if they are caught up in the opinions and fears of others. One of the biggest things that I learned from Pastor Joel Osteen is that other people's opinions of me are none of my business.

There were many people who came out of the woodwork who did not have my best interests at heart. I received letters from some people saying, "Steve, this is so devastating. How are you going to recover?" My publicist was trying to figure out how we were going to repair the damage. In prior years, people had told me that I was washed up after the Kings of Comedy tour. Before that, they said I was at rock bottom when my first radio show was canceled. Public relations experts told me my image would be ruined after my second divorce. I'm glad that God, not people, has the final say on a career. I've been blessed to have more than thirty-two years of working in an industry that I love.

To alleviate some of the emotional pain that I was in, I recited "Invictus." The whole poem, over and over. It saved me because it reflected what I was feeling—*I have not winced nor cried aloud. . . . My head is bloody, but unbowed.* I took what was being dished out. I had not winced or cried aloud.

Through the darkness there came some early light. I received calls from Tyler Perry, Joel Osteen, Magic Johnson, Cedric The Entertainer, Yolanda Adams, Kirk Franklin, Bishop T. D. Jakes, and Pastor Paula White. Dr. Phil reached out to offer advice on how to handle the situation, because he's done a ton of live television and recognized that what had happened was not a single-person mistake. I even got a surprise call from Halle Berry. We aren't close, but she just wanted to uplift me. As each one of them reached out to me, I told them, "Thank you. My head is up. My head is bloodied but unbowed." The Miss Universe adversity showed me who my real friends were. It showed me who would be there for me, who would help without my even asking. My real friends were there without hesitation.

When you get into trouble, you will not have to seek out your real true friends. They will come down and get in that hole with you. I did not have to call people and say, "Man, I got jacked up on this one. This one hurts." The very next morning after the incident, I received the longest text from Dr. Phil on how to handle it. He took me through it. I did not have to look for Bishop Jakes. Joel Osteen did not waste time. I heard from all of the "heavy ones" who honestly love me.

For five days, from December 20 to Christmas Day, it was just horrible. Death threats came. People rode by my house in SUVs, threatening to hurt my family. I could not let my children go anywhere. I had to have armed security guards at my gates. I got cursed out so many ways in Spanish that I thought I knew Spanish. I am certain that I can't vacation in Colombia anytime soon! I probably can't even drink Colombian coffee.

There was not only mayhem around my house; there were also protests in the streets of Colombia. They were even burning effigies. The Colombians felt they had been robbed of the crown as a country. The entire Latin community felt humiliated by the incident.

It's not uncommon after adversity hits for us to wallow in it to a degree, but we should not. I assure you that behind every moment of adversity there is a lesson and a blessing. The sooner I put the adversity behind me, the sooner I could receive my lesson from God. I have learned not to make past mistakes larger by focusing all my attention on them. I must look toward the next step in my life's journey. I realized that God had already gotten me through the mistake. There was no reason to keep it in front of me.

When I woke up on Christmas morning, I went outside by my pool. It was a sunny, sixty-degree day in Georgia. I sat down and lit a cigar. I held it up and had one of my sons take a picture of me. I posted a photo with a caption that read, "Merry Easter, y'all." By the end of Christmas week, that one post was being circulated more than all the other memes.

I started getting calls from friends and business partners who were as far away as France, Portugal, and Dubai. They offered their support in any way I needed it. I was beginning to see the blessings that had started to come from the adversity. A friend in Italy called me and said, "Man, I don't know what's going on, but you're on the front page of the paper here. Congratulations on doing the right thing. What an honor it is to know you."

Fast-forward to New Year's Day, and I was the most-talked-about person in the world. I was on the front page of many, many newspapers. I was getting praise from everywhere. The only one that was negative was a newspaper in Colombia—and it truly bothered me. I was sick to my stomach, not because of the mistake, but because I couldn't stop thinking about how Miss Colombia was feeling. It was tough on me, and at the same time, it could not compare with what Pia and Ariadna were going through. I have always been a champion of women, and I felt horrible that I had put them in this position.

I wanted to make it up to Miss Colombia and Miss Philippines. I did not know what I could do other than to apologize personally and hope that Ariadna Gutiérrez and Pia Wurtzbach would forgive me. I did not want to speak publicly about the incident until I gave each woman a chance to speak her truth. They were the most important people to be heard, as far as I was concerned.

I knew Miss Colombia was crushed. I'd seen it on her face at the pageant. I felt that she was humiliated and embarrassed. For weeks, I couldn't even get her on the phone. Her sister and her father were protecting her by intercepting my calls. As a father myself, I understood. I knew he had spent his entire life sheltering his daughter from pain. He was definitely not interested in allowing a man who had caused his daughter grief to reach her by phone.

At last, one day one of my producers said, "Ariadna wants to come on the show." I couldn't believe it. I was thrilled that I'd finally be able to talk to her face-to-face and apologize. After we had confirmed both of the women, we decided to do a two-part show to give them the time to fully express themselves. The shows were called "Miss Universe: The Truth."

Miss Philippines was the first guest. She was excited about being on the show. Having recently moved to New York since the pageant, she was enthusiastic about all of her new experiences in America. I was happy to see her, but my stomach was still doing flips. I was so nervous about her forgiveness. I was thankful that she gave me a warm hug. Pia expressed that when she was announced as the first runner-up, the excitement of the crowd comforted her. She recognized that her country was still proud of her for getting that far. After all, she had beat out seventy-nine other beautiful and talented women. She explained that when she realized that she was Miss Universe, she did not fully believe it. She had mixed feelings and a lot of concern for Ariadna, which is the reason she kept a respectful distance from her following the correction. During the night of the pageant, still in shock and disbelief, she asked her mother backstage if she had really won. When she replied yes, Pia asked if she was sure. Her mother said yes. That's when she had her Miss Universe moment.

At last, my opportunity to apologize to her, publicly, had arrived. I explained to her that I wished we could have gotten it right that night. I was relieved when she said, "Let's move forward. Let's be happy. It was a mistake. Let's not beat each other up for it." I felt like I could finally breathe. I needed her to know that I was sincerely sorry and how much her forgiveness meant to me.

"Miss Universe: The Truth, Part 2." Being named the most poised and accomplished woman in Colombia was second only to the presidency in terms of prestige in Ariadna's country. This was the moment I had been waiting for. It was my chance to make amends. I had been feeling horrible for almost a month. When Miss Colombia finally came out onstage, we hugged for a long time. It took everything in me not to cry right then and there. She was even more gorgeous than I remembered. Right away, I told her that I was incredibly sorry that my mistake had created such an uncomfortable and unfortunate situation for her. After Ariadna sat down on the set, she said, "I forgive you. I forgave you that night. I know you didn't mean to do it. That's not the way we rehearsed it." She even cracked a little joke. "I was Miss Universe for four and a half minutes!" Her face lit up with humor, and her beauty was even more obvious.

When Ariadna said, "I forgive you," it meant the world to me. It was what I so desperately needed to hear. I told her how much I appreciated her forgiveness and thanked her profusely. The last thing I ever wanted for her was to be bruised and hurt after the pageant. It was amazing to see her smiling and in a good place.

She told me that right after the pageant was over she ran to be with her family. She thanked them for being there since she was more worried about their feelings of disappointment than she was her own. She had to take a rest after all she had been through. At first, she blamed God, asking Him why He would do something like that to her. It took some time for her to believe that it had happened. When she got home, she watched a video of the show to confirm that it had indeed happened. Over the few days following the pageant, she spent time with her family to calm herself. She needed to sort out what she was going to do and say in response to what had happened. She felt like she was in a nightmare she couldn't wake up from.

It was fascinating to hear the lessons Ariadna and Pia had learned as a result of the events at the pageant. After Ariadna recovered somewhat, she realized that we all had to move on. The mishap was our collective destiny. She began to understand that everything happens for a reason, and that the reason for this event was to show her that her life would be bigger than being Miss Universe. The early evidence of this was the way she conducted herself during the situation. For starters, it made her a role model in Colombia. Looking on the bright side, she said that at the very least the pageant had given her three wonderful weeks in Las Vegas. Although the night of the pageant was the worst and the best night of her life, she was pleased that she got the opportunity to take a photograph with the crown. In the near future, she plans on working with the pageant.

I'm sure that great things will continue to happen in Ariadna's life because of her positive attitude. I told her that I hoped that God would use this moment to catapult her future success beyond her dreams.

We were both victimized by social media in the aftermath of the incident. In response, at the end of my television show we poked fun by laughing at our favorite memes. Ariadna closed with, *"Feliz Día de la Madre. Perdón . . . Feliz Navidad."* Translated, it means: "Happy Mother's Day. Sorry . . . Merry Christmas."

The Miss Universe experience reminded me to stay true to my core beliefs. I may be seen by many as successful. But the incident was a reminder from God that He can take it away at a moment's notice. However, because I have faith in Him and His power, I conducted myself in a way that the Bible says is the best way to Glory. I spoke the truth. I took responsibility, I sat still, and I waited for his guidance. I jumped at the opportunity to set the record straight, without thinking about what I had to lose.

Everybody has a Miss Universe moment, and how you handle that moment of adversity is by simply choosing to do the right thing. It is a promise of God that when you do the right thing, an even better thing will happen. It is true; I have found it to be true that if you take one step, He'll take two. When you are bold enough to step off in faith, to jump, that is when you'll soar.

We have to be still to hear from God. However, you do not want to be so still that you become complacent. Other than in moments of crisis, I sometimes also sit still when I find myself so caught up in work that I ask, "Wait a minute, I'm really busy, but am I being productive? I'm not seeing the needle moving. I have been spinning my wheels, but what am I doing wrong?" It's under circumstances such as this that I will sit still and

It is a promise of God that when you do the right thing, an even better thing will happen. . . . If you take one step, He'll take two. When you are bold enough to step off in faith, to jump, that is when you'll soar.

wait for direction. Other than that, I am in perpetual motion, moving toward God's next plan for me.

I live my life expecting the good in everything. I am always looking for the blessing. I am ever optimistic and searching for the next great thing that God has for me. My motto is "Always be closing." I tell my radio audience that: Always be closing. That's because I'm always on the move, jumping to close a new deal. I believe important lessons are always followed by blessings. This was the case after the Miss Universe incident. A few weeks later, I got a call from T-Mobile. They wanted me to star in a commercial mocking what had happened at the pageant. And they wanted to air the commercial during the Super Bowl! Come Super Bowl Sunday, the commercial was one of the top two commercials of the night. That opportunity came off the heels of adversity. I couldn't have ever imagined that happening. God took something that many people deemed bad and turned it into something amazing.

For the past few years, one of my requests during my morning gratitude prayers was for God to increase my global presence. To that end, I started aligning with people who were developing businesses to improve the trade, roads, and infrastructure in Africa. I thought that by connecting myself with these people I could help the continent in a meaningful way. I had no idea that God would use this devastating moment from the Miss Universe pageant to help me with this goal of broadening my global reach. God had used this moment of adversity to help me with my goal.

When I asked God to expand my global persona, I was simply considering actions within my control that I could work on and develop with my team. I have been shown more than a few times that what I dream and think about is just a fraction of what God really has in store for me. The goals I put on my vision board are often just the start of the dream.

In those five days after the pageant, I'll be honest, I wasn't sure how all of it was going to play out. There were a few times when I didn't know if this one moment would affect my ability to keep doing what I loved to do. God, who has brought me through every single situation in my life, again did not let me down. And He won't let you down when you make your big jump either.

4

Life Is
a Four-Letter
Word

Understand that when you fail, you are in the midst of a great lesson.

You must put your hopes in motion, and God will bless your steps if you are taking some.

Life is a series of lessons learned and failures overcome.

Though you may not know exactly what your journey will be to bring you to your dream, be open to the process, and seize the opportunities God presents to you.

I had recently gotten married to Marjorie when I found out that my longtime accountant had died. I felt horrible and was saddened by his untimely death. When I discovered that he had not filed my taxes for seven years, I was in shock. For seven whole years I hadn't paid a dime to the IRS, even though each year I'd sent him a check for my taxes. He never cashed the checks or filed my returns. I saw all those checks and returns on his desk, and my heart dropped. By the time my manager and I went through all the paperwork and learned that between non-filing fees and penalties, I owed so much money I could not think straight—over eight figures!

I had married Marjorie. I had seven children and a new wife who were depending on me. We had four teenagers at the time, whom we eventually wanted to put through college.

I was intimidated by the tax bill, but I was mostly worried about breaking the news to Marjorie. We had just said our vows—for better, for worse, for richer, for poorer—and the first thing we had to face as a couple was owing the IRS that type of money, which we didn't have. We started our marriage in a financial hole. I was worried that she would think I wasn't able to take care of our family, or that I was not the man she thought I was or that she needed me to be. It was one of the toughest conversations of my life to have to tell her. I had just found the woman of my dreams, we'd just blended our families and moved to a new state, and we were now faced with a devastating financial situation so early in our marriage.

I had buddies and people on my team who said, "Steve, don't tell her. It's better that she doesn't know." But I knew I could not do that. As Slick Harvey's son, I knew that I wouldn't be able to face myself as a man if I didn't come clean to her.

My father set a strong example for me and my brothers about how to be a good father and husband. He never let our family down. My father always made sure that we were covered and protected. I remember distinctly, when I was a little boy, probably around age eight or so, standing there waiting for my mother to pull on her coat for our bus ride downtown. My father came in the room and said, very simply, "You and your mother are going downtown—watch out for your mother." That was rule number one in my father's house. "Take care of your mother." So growing up I knew that as a man one of my most important responsibilities was to protect the women in my life—my mother, my sisters, and my wife.

Although I couldn't imagine what Marjorie's response would be, I knew there was no way I could be anything less than completely honest with her by owning up to the problem. I just thought, "If this woman leaves me over this, I will be the most surprised man on earth." I had faith in God. I told her about the bill and what it would mean for us financially.

You will have to purchase most of the hard, meaningful lessons in your life. And they will be expensive. The lessons I was about to learn were going to cost tens of millions. It doesn't mean that you will always have to pay for your lesson in cash, but trust me, you will have to pay with something valuable—time, opportunities lost, or an inconvenience of some kind. It's necessary to understand that when we fail big, while we're in the center of the disaster, we're in the midst of our greatest lesson.

After I sat down with Marjorie and explained that we were in a lot of trouble, she cried. It was her way of getting ready for us to go to work. Marjorie is the kind of person who cries to get it out of her system and then goes to work in addressing the issue. She stayed right by my side. When a tax adviser told me it would take at least twelve years to dig out of that hole, she stayed. When I told her just how hard I would have to work and how often I would be away from home, she promised me that she would continue to be my rock.

It's awful to wake up and feel like you can't take care of your family how you want to. I was not deterred. I had experienced all kinds of money issues in my life. I have been in every economic situation you can be in. I've been dirt poor. I've been homeless. I've lived check to check. At each of those challenging moments in my life, I kept my faith, and it saw me through. This new problem would be no different.

I got my plan together to pay off the debt. I have always been committed to a strong work ethic. I was no stranger to hard work. I come from a family of hard workers. My father gave me my work ethic. I watched him work hard every day. He worked first as a coal miner because that's the type of work he could get in rural West Virginia. Then he started working in construction, and eventually became a foreman.

I was cut from the same cloth. The only time I'm ever still is when I am on vacation and need to recharge my batteries. That is the only time I am intentionally not productive. When I go to bed at night I recharge my batteries, but I'm right back at it the next day. I believe that if I take one step, God will take two. So why would I not keep stepping? If I'm doing one and He's doing two, I'm going to get along a lot faster than not taking any steps. But often people will put all the pressure on God. "I don't know why God isn't blessing me," they'll say. Yet they haven't given

> *God can bless your steps if you are taking some. He cannot bless your steps if you are not taking any.*

God anything to bless. God can bless your steps if you are taking some. He cannot bless your steps if you are not taking any. "Oh Lord, I can't find a job!" You pray and lament, yet you haven't left the house! I believe in putting my hope in motion. You gotta give God something to work with!

Aside from being away from my family, I did not feel any way about taking on the extra work. I was willing to take on any and every job available. I worked every Friday and every Saturday. I was on the road more than I was home. Marjorie held it down while I was out there hustling. In my absence, leaving Marjorie alone with our children, I essentially made her a single parent at times. I was confident in her dedication to me, and I never felt alone while I was on the road. I knew that if she could stand with me through owing all this money, she'd stand with me through anything.

To pay down the tax bill, I basically lived at the airport during the first few years of our marriage as I traveled from city to city making appearances and hosting gigs. My goal was to pay off the bill in less than twelve years. And I jumped on it. I could not wait to get on the other side of the tax bill.

To be honest, I was fearful about the tax debt. I knew there were people who had gone to jail for not filing taxes. I went back to the hustle-and-grind mentality: Inch by inch, everything's a cinch. I knew that I had no singular resource that could get me out of this much tax debt. There was no one job, no one gig, that would get me out of it. I tried the shotgun approach. I started signing an accumulation of contracts for everything presented to me—book deals, game show deals, whatever it was. But my most important resource was that I was a stand-up comedian and could sell out an arena anywhere in the country. I took every single gig available to me. I worked myself raggedy rag. If the gig couldn't pay my asking price, I found out what was the best the venue could do and I did it for that. I was flexible. "Because we can't give you $150,000, would you take $120,000." "Yes I will." "Will you take $90,000 this week?" "Yes I will." "Will you do Friday here for $80,000? And then go here for $75,000 on Saturday?" "Yes I will." I kept stacking and packing, doing gigs, speaking engagements, appearances. I didn't care what it was. I took everything to the point where Marjorie said you've got to slow down.

I couldn't slow down because I couldn't see anything but the tax payments. I stayed tight. It was a nerve-wracking period. In my home office, I had a big window that faced toward the front of my house. I could see the gate where people entered in clear view. Every time the gate opened or the bell rang, I was sure it was somebody from the sheriff's department coming to put me in jail. I lived in a nightmare of concern and worry. Did I miss the payment? Did they change their mind about our agreement? Did somebody at the IRS office get our payment arrangement mixed up? Are they coming to put stickers on the door? I knew so many friends who had their cars confiscated, boats chained up, by the government. I just worried all the time. It was like being on a tight rope going over Niagara Falls with no net, no harness, no pole. A gust of wind could have just blown me over.

It was also crippling my lifestyle. Everything I did, I had to have the tax payments in mind. If I bought a pair of boots. If Marjorie shopped. If we tried to get away for a minute for a trip. It was all determined by whether or not I had made the payment for the month. I was told very clearly that I could not miss one single payment.

Nobody knew what I was going through internally with the tax debt hanging over me. It felt like I was in a blinding abyss. It was like being in a blizzard and you can't see. I just kept my head up and faced it. *My head is bloody, but unbowed.* Scriptures kept me going, too. *You will walk through the rivers and they will not overcome you. You will walk through the fire and not get burned. No kindling will set upon your clothing.* Everything I had learned up until that point had to come into play—to never give up, keep the faith, and don't let any man outwork you. I had the faith that I would somehow get through it, even though the payments were incredibly daunting. It required every single thing I had to pull us out of that.

Then, a miracle came along. I sold 49 percent of my radio company to Clear Channel. And I was able to pay off eight more years' worth of scheduled tax payments with one stroke of a pen after struggling with payments for four years. December 28, 2012, I was free. I was free—finally.

I refuse to think that anything that ever happens to me is final. The only way anything can happen to me that is final is if I don't wake up. Other than that, it is not final. I have faith in God. I didn't know how He was going to do it, but I had trusted that God would get me through the storm. He has never let me down.

> *God doesn't put you in a dark place forever. He has never not gotten you through something.*

Life is a series of lessons learned and failures overcome. I knew that once I embraced the tax problem, I would learn something valuable. God doesn't put you in a dark place forever. He has never *not* gotten you through something.

A Journey and a Jump

In 1995, when I was finding my footing in the entertainment industry, I became an entrepreneur. I opened a comedy club in Dallas, Texas, where I was living at the time, called Steve Harvey's Comedy House. I started the club for comedians, but I had a wide range of poets, entertainers, and up-and-coming actors and singers perform there, among them Erykah Badu. She worked at the Comedy House when she was twenty-three and still in college at Grambling State.

Erykah had just started her journey toward the bright star she is today when she began working at the Comedy House. When we first met she was rapping and emceeing a lot with Free, who went on to become a popular host on BET's *106 and Park*. Erykah started as a waitress, and because of her wit, engaging personality, and style, she quickly became our hostess. She then moved to the ticket booth. I trusted her implicitly to handle the money and to help organize transportation and hotel reservations for the comedians who came in. She was so good at it that she came to me and created the position of stage manager, making sure everybody was taken care of. One day I was late going onstage, so Erykah went out to the mic and told some jokes and stuff to give me time to get there. People were laughing and heckling and having fun, and when I arrived and went onstage, I playfully scolded her for trying to take that job, too. The whole place cracked up. We started doing it several nights.

Erykah was open to all the opportunities to use her gift. Unlike me, she didn't think she was someone who could make people laugh. I don't think she knew she could entertain. But when she had to step in, she did. She jumped at the opportunity to use her gift to connect with people from the stage. She has gone on to utilize her God-given talents in many ways—as a poet, a singer, and an activist. She helps shape and mentor young people with her straight talks. Because she seized the moment on the stage that night, she unlocked her gift. She jumped, and she's been jumping ever since.

You don't have to know exactly what your journey will be or the steps that will bring you to your dream—just be open to the process, be open to the path. Seize the opportunities God presents to you even if they don't seem directly related to your dream. That day in the '90s, Erykah didn't know she would be taking a step on her path to being an entertainer. Her reason for jumping that night was not even about her dream. Her work responsibilities forced her to jump. She was simply doing what had to be done, and in doing so, she was blessed to understand her gift a little more deeply.

Another way to see jumping is to view it as a climb: At each rung you will learn something that prepares you for the next level of your life. And at each level you will become stronger and better able to handle defeat, detours, or setbacks. Every rung will put you in a more rewarding position to receive blessings.

As I said earlier, the first major jump in my life was on October 8, 1985—I jumped from being an insurance salesmen to becoming a stand-up comedian.

My next big jump wasn't conscious. Chuck Sutton, who was my boss at *Showtime at the Apollo*, had called the Montreal Comedy Festival and told them about me. "We've never heard of him." "You will if you put him on." Next thing you know, I got an invitation to do the festival. Of course, I didn't have the money to go. It was not one of those gigs where they paid your way.

Fortunately, Chuck Sutton gave me an advance against my pay.

I flew to Montreal to do the Just for Laughs comedy festival. "Danger Night" they called it. You have to write ten minutes' worth of jokes and it can't be material. You have to make up stuff on the spot. That's what I do. I walked in that night and I wasn't playing with them. I was eating them alive. Montreal is a French-speaking city. I went up there and talked about walking around Montreal, not being able to speak French. They were screaming. They could tell it wasn't material because I was talking about the stuff around me.

On the first night some guys from ABC were in the audience. They came backstage to meet me. "You are brilliantly funny!" one of them said.

Two days later they invited me over to their hotel. They asked me if I could act. I told them yeah, despite the fact that I had never been in a school play or acted a day in my life. They pitched me a television show called *Me and the Boys*. It was about a single dad with three boys. By Friday, they wrote me a check for a $50,000 holding deal. I took their offer and jumped.

I needed to move to Los Angeles, where we would work on the pilot. They gave me a $10,000 moving fee. I took it, even though I didn't have any furniture or anything big to move. I just had clothes and I didn't have many of those. I used the money to put a down payment on an apartment.

I got set up on the West Coast and we began shooting the pilot. Madge Sinclair was my mother-in-law on the show. They gave me a script, and I wasn't sure exactly how it was to be used. I thought the executives wanted the guy they saw onstage in Montreal, so I approached it like it was material. *And Steve crosses to the refrigerator. Reaches up and gets the bread. As he says morning mama how you doing today.* I was reading everything on the page, stage directions included.

I'm sure the television people were mortified to see that I didn't know how to act.

But I didn't notice it because I'm doing the dude onstage. One of the extras on the show was Cassi Davis of *Tyler Perry's House of Payne*. She's also done several movies. She's from Holly Springs, Mississippi. She's a church girl. She approached me:

"Brother, can I talk to you for a moment? Can I tell you something since you're from the country, too? Listen to me. Look at me when I'm talking to you. If you don't get yourself together and learn how to talk like a regular person and learn how to act, they're going to take this money away from you."

Now, keep in mind, that was the most money I had seen in my life at that point, regardless that I was the lowest-paid person who was a lead on a television show anywhere on TV. I was making $50,000 a week. I was paid the lowest because I didn't know what to charge. Fifty thousand a week was the most I had heard of anybody in my world making. I took it.

Cassi said, "They're going to take this money away from you if you don't learn to act."

You think I'm about to let them take this $50,000 away from me? I hadn't ever had $50,000 in my life. You going to give me this every Thursday? And now you talking about taking it. You gots to be kidding. Where else was I going to get $50,000 from? I couldn't get no $50,000 a night telling jokes, not in 1993. That wasn't happening.

Wasn't no way in hell I could let that happen. "I can figure this out by tomorrow morning."

"No you can't," she said.

"Yes I can if they're going to take $50,000 from me. How am I supposed to talk?"

"Regular like these were your sons. How would you tell them?"

"I would tell them go on in there and get your coat."

"How would your father tell you?"

"Well, we couldn't do that on television!"

"Listen to me. Kim Fields's mama is an acting coach." I knew of Kim Fields as Tootie on *The Facts of Life*. "I'm going to ask her to come by your hotel tonight and work on the script with you. Because tomorrow you got to get yourself together because the TV people are just looking at you. They can't believe they have made this mistake."

Chip Fields came to my room that night. We stayed up all night. I memorized lines. She was throwing all kinds of stuff at me. The next day when I came on the set, the producers couldn't believe it. I saw their mouths hanging open.

I told the show people that she was my acting coach, and they offered to pay for my lessons. They were willing to do anything. Chip formally became my acting coach the next day. She was even on the set coaching me. By the time we shot the pilot, I could act a little bit and had developed levels. After about two weeks, she said, "You don't need me no more. I ain't never seen anybody get it like this. Just be yourself."

After a pretty successful run, the network canceled *Me and the Boys*. It was the highest-rated show to be canceled in ABC history. However, Matt Williams was the creator of *Home Improvement*, the number one show that season. And in his contract it was stated that if he finished the season in the top ten he could take the time slot following his show, which was mine. *Me and the Boys* finished number 21.

ABC then offered me a $75,000 signing bonus to do a new show. I wouldn't sign it. I needed $300,000. I wanted to buy a house and I wanted $1 million. Because I didn't have good credit, the only way I could get the house was to put down $300,000. My mortgage would be $2,500. I knew that I could hustle that on the road. My agent, Fred Whitehead, didn't think it was possible for me to get that kind of money. He said the largest bonus was given to Don Johnson, and that was $400,000. Why would they give me $300,000?

"Because I'm going to ask" was my response.

I went to the office of the chairman, Ted Harbert. He's the one who had put me on *Me and the Boys.* His assistant said that he was not there and that he couldn't see me. I told her, I'll wait. I stayed at ABC walking in the hallways, waiting. Finally, I saw Ted in the hallway.

"Hello, Steve, what's going on? What are you doing here?"

"I'm here to talk to you. I know you're trying to give me a $75,000 signing bonus, but I can't take that."

"Well, why not, Steve?"

"Because I need $300,000."

"Whoa!"

"Look man, I had a hit show and you took me off of TV. If I don't get nothing else out of this deal, I need a house."

"Are you kidding me? Where's your agent?"

"He doesn't think I should ask for it."

"Who is your agent?"

"Fred Whitehead."

"So, you're in here negotiating your own deal."

"Yeah, he don't get it. I don't need him anyway. I need you."

"Come back tomorrow at four p.m."

The next day, he handed me a check for $300,000. I bought a house in Texas. I've been hustling for houses ever since.

I've always loved radio. I got my start on WGCI in Chicago. I would sit up there all day promoting the comedy club. And the club sold out every week. One day, the late great Doug Banks (one of the greatest radio guys in all of radio) asked me to do him a favor. He asked me to sit in for him one afternoon. I did it from two to six. I was talking to people, taking live phone calls, playing jams, running jokes. The people went crazy. The phones were lit. I ended up sitting in two days in a row. Doug Banks gave me my first crack. He said, "All jokes aside, man you funny." The next thing you know Elroy Smith asked, "Have you ever thought about doing radio?"

I said, "No."

"You'd be great at it."

I signed a contract.

Next thing you know I was the morning man in Chicago. I did it for a year.

About this time, ABC sold my contract to a new network, The WB. They were looking for some stars. I wasn't no real star, but they figured if I had a hit show on one network, I was a good bet. The WB sent two people to see me, Winifred Hervey and Stan Lathan. They came to Chicago and said we have a TV show and we think you can become a TV star.

"Really, what is it?"

"You're going to be a high school teacher in an inner-city school. They were talking to me about being a math teacher. They asked what I knew about. I told them that I could play keyboard a little bit. I used to be a lot better when I played all the time. I sat down and hit some chords for them. They said we'll make you a music teacher.

They asked what name would I like to use on the sitcom. I remembered this dude, Lonnie Hightower, back in school. I used to love his name: Lonnie Hightower. I told them I wanted to be Steve Hightower. It was a play on names from my first show. On *Me and the Boys*, I owned a video store and I was Steve Tower.

They invited me out to shoot the pilot. They told me that I was going to have a friend on the show. They suggested George Wendt, the dude who was Norm on *Cheers*. I told them I had someone in mind, Cedric The Entertainer from St. Louis. He's funny. He would be more my friend. They said, Wendt was a star. You want the show to be funny or to have stars on it, was my question to them. We went back and forth. "We've never heard of Cedric The Entertainer." So what. I told them ain't nobody ever heard of me either. After some convincing, they brought him out for test. They didn't like him. They insisted that they wanted to put Wendt on the show. I told them that I would pass. I wouldn't do it unless Ced's on board. I wanted to work with a dude I knew and liked. Two weeks later they called back and said that they signed Cedric.

I flew back out there and we shot the pilot. It was a huge hit.

No matter what job I was doing, in my heart, I was a stand-up comedian. I never wanted to be anything else. Although I did the TV show, I never considered myself an actor, and every weekend I went on the road to perform. I thought of the TV show as my side hustle. In fact, everything that I did outside of touring

I put on the sideline. I felt this way about all of my TV shows—*Family Feud*, the talk show, *The Steve Harvey Show*, *Steve Harvey's Big Time*, *Me and the Boys*. Even all the specialty shows, such as the BET Awards. (Me and Ced hosted the first two BET Awards shows.) I felt this way up until I retired from stand-up on August 15, 2012. But every time somebody offered me something else I jumped. I did it. I went for it. I've never been afraid to reinvent myself. I've always been looking for another way toward the life God has planned for me.

Opportunities on the big screen came next. I did *Racing Stripes*, *The Fighting Temptations*, *You Got Served*, and *Johnson Family Vacation*. I never auditioned for any of these movies. Someone asked me to do them. Ced asked me to be in *Johnson Family Vacation* with him. The casting people for *Racing Stripes* called me to play the part of Buzz the fly. For *You Got Served*, Chris Stokes called me to play Mr. Rad. An English director cast me in *The Fighting Temptations* without a reading. I never wanted to be a movie star. My heart was not in it. I tried it, but I wanted to be on TV, not in the movies.

In about year five of *The Steve Harvey Show*, Walter Latham came to me and Ced with a proposition. He wanted to tour me, Cedric, and Bernie Mac. We were all selling three thousand, five thousand seaters, depending on the city. Ced's comedy career was big. Bernie's was big off of *Def Comedy Jam*. Walter's idea was to bring our comedy to arenas.

We looked at him and said, "We're going to do what, dog?"

"Arenas."

"What do you mean arenas?"

"Where they play basketball," he said.

"We're going to tell jokes where they play basketball?"

"How many seats is that?"

"Minimum sixteen thousand."

I said, "Man, you gots to be kidding. Can't nobody do that."

"I'll pay you $150,000 a night, plus bonuses."

"What kind of bonus you talking about?"

"We sell out and you can walk out of there with $275,000 a night."

"Two hundred seventy-five thousand dollars telling jokes!?

He came back later: "I got eighteen cities."

When God puts something in your imagination,
you have to run with it. You can't let anybody
kill the vision that God puts inside you.

Eighteen cities!!!

I started doing the math: $200,000 multiplied by eighteen cities. I told him that I needed a deposit. I was thinking if he could give me a deposit it could work. About ten days later, before the first gig, he gave me a $200,000 deposit. He handed me a check for a lot of money to tell jokes. *The Kings of Comedy* was an exciting and lucrative endeavor. It was well worth the jump!

I rarely quote rappers, but Biggie Smalls was right— "mo' money, mo' problems." Several years ago, after the first few seasons of *Family Feud* and after the first season of *The Steve Harvey Show*, I had a business associate close to me in my camp say, "You have to be careful about spreading yourself too thin." I highly valued this person's opinion. And what he said did not change my view of his talents. However, I had to recognize that he simply did not share in my vision. When God puts something in your imagination, you have to run with it. You can't let anybody kill the vision that God puts inside you. My vision had become much bigger than my associate. The things I was imagining were larger than their perspective.

As I sat down and began to tell him that I was going to branch off into bigger opportunities within entertainment and larger ventures outside entertainment, he started giving me pushback that was disguised as good advice. My associate was afraid that I would spread myself too thin and overexpose myself. He was more worried about how this could affect his livelihood than he was concerned about having faith in me and my abilities.

People automatically think that when you spread yourself out in new directions, you are spreading yourself thin. That's not always true. When you give yourself the room to see how far you can jump, you give yourself more opportunities to share your gift and to help others do the same.

You can't be afraid to spread your gift beyond your imagination and comfort zone. You've heard people say, "I never imagined that I'd be here." But, they're there because somewhere along the way, they took a chance on an unfamiliar path. Somewhere they stepped out of their comfort zone. Spreading the gifts that God gave you doesn't lessen their value. When God gives you more opportunities to show who you are and to provide greater value to the world, that's your moment to better understand how to use your gift and also to empower the people around you to further expand your vision and theirs.

About fifteen years ago, I had a fellow comedian ask me if I could help him out with a gig. He and I were cool. We would hang out every now and again, and he was a good comedian with a decent set. At the time, I was doing a fifteen-city summer comedy tour. These were venues with fifteen hundred to two thousand seats in smaller cities, but my promoter was doing a great job of selling out my shows in every market. I was midway through the tour when he asked and I said, "Okay, man. I'll throw you a bone." I agreed to let him come on the road as an opening act for $1,500 a night.

The night before this comedian is scheduled to come on tour with me, he calls and says, "Hey man, I'm gonna need more money." I said, "Why?" He had the nerve to reply, "Because I'm worth more than that." His name wasn't on the tickets, the posters, or the marquees. I was doing him a favor by allowing him to put some money in his pocket on my tour. He ended the call with, "Man, just call me when you figure out how much you can give me. And I'm gonna need $3,500 for tonight."

I couldn't believe he did this the night before we were set to go out on tour. Before I could get too upset,

I spoke with my promoter. He said he had a young man who was just starting out, and was willing to take the same opening gig for $500 a night. My promoter said, "Steve, he would love to go with you. He just wants to be around you and learn." I hired him on the spot and kept my tour moving. Needless to say, that other comedian never got a call back about his $3,500 a night.

Can you believe, I ran into him a few years later after I started my sitcom? He said, "Man, you gotta put me on your show." I responded, "I don't have a place for you." Then he starts calling everybody from my attorney to my publicist to my manager. I finally got on the phone with him and said, "Brother, listen to me. I've never met anyone who is more ungrateful and two-faced than you. I don't owe you nothing." All he could say was, "Man, you've changed."

He was right—I had changed. I had changed so much that I no longer felt responsible for carrying him or anyone else who believed that they were entitled to my success. I had changed to the point where I knew that I didn't have to live up to anyone's expectations of who they thought I should be. So when people say, "You've changed," it's okay, because change is a good thing.

One thing Magic Johnson said to me that stuck with me was, "Most people aren't up in the clouds; they

don't know how hard it is to breathe up here." They
don't know how thin the air is. It's you climbing Mount
Everest. You need people around you who have been
climbing up in this airspace, to show you how to catch
your breath. The majority of people don't finish their
climb to Mount Everest. I watched a television special
and it claimed that there are still bodies up there right
now. But you've got people on the ground with radios
to help you get there and back. That's your support
team. Magic is on my team. He always has a radio to
help me get back down to the ground.

The higher you climb in life and the more you
attain, the fewer people you will have to count on. As
you get to the top of wherever you are on your journey,
there will be fewer people doing the things that you are
doing. Does that mean you are supposed to be afraid
of climbing? No. You have to make your journey up to
the top.

5

A Man Without a Vision or a Dream Shall Perish

Happiness is having a purpose in life.

*Your dream has to be tied to something that
you are gifted at doing.*

*Every victory should be a confidence booster
to let you know that even more is possible.*

*Once you get a few victories under your belt,
you can keep building your vision and making
your dreams even bigger.*

*No matter what you are going through,
you can change your life.*

I have this image in my phone—there's a massive male lion and a little cub behind him. The caption reads, "I thought about quitting but I realized who was watching me." When I think about my children, I see those words in my mind. I've had moments of weakness. I don't want anybody to think that I'm just this big, brave soldier. Sometimes the enemy looks so much bigger than me. Sometimes the battle feels un-winnable. But when I look behind me and I see my children looking at me, I cannot allow them to see me quit. They can see me fail—and they've had to watch that several times—but they can't ever see me quit. That's not an option for them to see their father quit. They can see me fail, but they can't ever see me quit. They can see me killing myself trying, but they can't ever see me quit.

When they see me, they see one of the hardest-working people they know. And I'm willing to work harder if necessary. My sons have a front-row seat to what a real work ethic is, to what you can achieve if you don't give up. They can't say that they don't know what it takes to make it. Now, I don't want my sons to see the example I've put in front of them and say something like, "I don't think I can live up to my daddy" or "I don't think I can fill your shoes." I've never asked for my sons to fill my shoes. I just tell them to put on their shoes and get to walking.

That's what I do every day—I don't quit and I work my butt off to achieve my goals. What wakes me up every day is the realization that there's so much more work to do that I haven't done yet. And the older I get, the more I recognize that. Happiness for me is living a life of purpose. I don't see how a person could be happy without a purpose or mission. The scripture says, "A man without a vision or a dream shall perish."

After my shows, many young men would come up to talk to me. Each and every one of them asked for advice about following their dreams, building strong relationships, and networking. And almost all of them asked if I had any job opportunities. They were willing to do anything. I was flattered that they felt I was someone they could relate to and someone they thought enough of to ask for guidance. I knew there had to be a way to let these young men know that there were men around who cared about them and their future.

But as it says in the Bible, to whom much is given, much is required. You never know what will motivate you to take on your next big dream. Meeting these impressionable young men inspired me to jump by starting a mentoring camp.

> *As it says in the Bible, to whom much is given, much is required.*

The camp started out as a vision to get young men out of their everyday environment and into a positive space where they could learn how to do better and how to be better. It would be a place where they could be mentored by men they could relate to, who had come from their neighborhoods and had grown up in the types of home they were still in, who had been where they are now, and who had made a success of their life. My goal was to give direction to boys who didn't have a father figure at home, to help create a generation of men who were emotionally, socially, and financially strong, in order to help strengthen the overall community. As a father, I know how important it is to have a strong male figure in your life. The lessons I learned from my father as I was growing up have been invaluable in molding me into a man who is able to face adversity and to persevere despite it. I wanted to pass their guidance on to the young men coming up today.

Initially, I didn't know how it was going to come together. But, when we haven't done something before, we rarely do. It began with hope, which I followed up with research. I needed to find out what the business would require.

Do you have the talent for what you are hoping for? Do you have the gift for what you are hoping for? See, you can quit hoping to be in the NBA if you are forty. There are no forty-year-old NBA players. You're not going to the league at forty. Let's make sure that what you are hoping for, you have the talent for or the gift to do, because it has to be tied to one of those two things or else it is a futile hope. What if someone says he hopes to jump to the moon one day. Okay, you hope to do what? You can do squats and by the time your legs are built enough after all them years you probably will not be able to jump there no how. Your hope has to be tied to something that you're gifted at or have a talent for and is in the realm of reality.

Embracing hope and faith, I began small. I jumped by moving toward my dream; I used the power of forward motion—the power of swinging my ax, the power of taking the next step. I used the resources at my disposal and grew my dream from there. Initially, I did not have sponsors on board with the camp. I decided that in order to propel my vision forward, I would put my own money into the camp. As the host of a national morning radio show, I put out a call to action to my listening audience to solicit applications to the camp. I used my personal relationships within my fraternity and businesses to seek mentors. I had a property in Dallas, Texas, that I was not able to enjoy throughout the year as much as I would have liked to, and I decided to make that the location for the camp. I wanted these young men to experience this property because it holds such a special place in my heart. A picturesque backdrop amid acres of green trees resting right on a lake, making it ideal for fishing and swimming—two activities many of the boys had never done growing up in urban environments. I did not even realize how much I already had at my disposal. God had already laid the foundation; I just needed to show up and do my part. Inch by inch, everything's a cinch.

No business starts by generating $100 million in revenue out of the gate. You start with one product or one idea. Coca-Cola began with one formula for a can of cola. Apple began with one home computer. The Wright brothers began with their hope of putting a plane in the sky.

What is the one idea that you can begin with today? What is the one service that you can do better than anyone else? What is that one product that you know everybody loves? You need only one solid idea to make that jump.

My goal was singular: I wanted to bring young men into a safe place and share valuable life lessons. I wanted to send these boys back to their communities, back into the world better than when they arrived. The camp opened in Dallas, Texas, in June 2009. To my surprise, more than five thousand young men applied to camp that year. I was thinking we would have something like fifty or so young men. When those original one hundred boys arrived on-site, it just blew my mind. I almost could not believe we were really making this happen. We even had sponsors that donated everything from money to books to clothing items for the boys. Athletes and entertainers wanted to come and share their own gifts and talents with the boys. As I stood there and watched them pour into the camp, I knew that it would be a powerful weekend.

The mentors and I discussed with them how their present choices could affect their lives and their futures and how their behavior in the street represents their families. We talked about the importance of education and how to make better decisions about their school-work. We discussed how their involvement in the community, and how they were treating the women in their lives, would shape them for years to come. We talked about their dreams and how to work toward them. We covered the basics, too. We taught them how to tie a tie and the benefits of nutrition and physical fitness, and why it's important to take pride in their communities, in their homes, and in themselves. There were young men who never had an older man in their life to show them how to properly knot a tie or how to shave. We helped them feel more confident about becoming a man. Our goal is to help these young men to recognize that they have to be extraordinary at whatever they do. We tell these young men that they should not settle for being regular. Regular people get regular pay, live regular lives, and end up with regular results.

By the end of that first weekend, we saw smiles coming from young men who had walked through the door with a chip on their shoulders. We saw a light in the eyes of young men who had walked in looking lost. When those first one hundred boys walked out of that camp, I knew that their lives had changed forever. Mine had, too. I knew I had to find a way to keep the program going. I didn't know how we would do it, we didn't have the money, the facilities, or the outreach, but I had faith that this was an opportunity in my life to make a difference and to empower so many young men, who needed only to know that someone loved them and cared about them.

I reached out to everyone and anyone I thought would help with the camp. Men who I knew cared about our community and our young men. My daughter Brandi helped contact organizations to get more sponsorships and even more boys to apply to the camp. That following year we even began hosting our annual fundraising gala in New York. Before we could even start up for that second summer, we had more corporate donors than before, and some of the biggest names in sports and entertainment were wanting to lend their support. My good friend Denzel Washington not only came to camp that year, but along with his lovely wife, Pauletta, made a sizable donation to fuel our efforts.

In the years that followed, we've had young men who've showed up on the brink of being kicked out of school and some who were a step away from prison. There were young men who came to the camp after being physically abusive to their family and to members of their community. We've even had teenage fathers looking for direction and guidance for their own children. If these young men could see upstanding, mature men in action doing the right things, they could have a shot at a brighter future. We bring them to the camp to learn, grow, and understand what they can be, and to discover that thing that God has created them to do. It would take more than a weekend to undo some of the things these young men have been through. But I knew from the lessons that I learned from my own father—responsibility, drive, focus—that a positive male influence can have an impact in ways that can last a lifetime.

Who would have thought that I would grow up and be something? I'm the youngest of five and my father was a coal miner. If I try to explain my life today, I can't explain how I got here. God is just so amazing. I had a dream to be one TV since I was nine years old, and I didn't actually get on TV until I was thirty-eight. I found what I was passionate about and I married it to my gift.

No matter what level you are on, whether you are a CEO with a seven-figure salary or an aspiring entrepreneur with a great idea, you have to appreciate every accomplishment along the way. Every victory should be a confidence booster to let you know that even more is possible. Once you get a few victories under your belt, you can keep building on your vision and making your dreams even bigger. That's what we did with the mentoring camp. We kept building on the success of that first year.

Now, seven years later, we have more than two hundred boys come to the camp for a full week to be mentored by positive male role models who are leaders in business, their communities, the entertainment industry, and the United States Armed Forces. We have also created a week- long camp for the single mothers of our boys to give them tools to become better parents and to strengthen the bond with their sons. The camp has become popular, and I have celebrities coming up to me and asking how they can participate. Over the last seven years of hosting the mentoring camp, we've had mentors who have included the educator Dr. Steve

Perry, the actor and television host Terrence J, Yolanda Adams, and Iyanla Vanzant.

Along with helping the kids, another blessing that has come as a result of creating the camp is bringing the mentors together. Most of the mentors return each year, and we have bonded in incredible ways. We support each other emotionally, as well as sometimes work on projects together outside the camp. For example, Terrence J starred in *Think Like A Man*, produced by Will Packer. The film was an adaptation of my *New York Times* bestselling book *Act Like a Lady, Think Like a Man*. I practice what I preach. I want to be able to give young creative minds an opportunity to showcase their talent and pay it forward.

My family also works for the camp. I'm continually impressed with how hard my children work. My daughter Brandi serves as the executive director of the foundation and takes on much of the responsibility in ensuring the camps are run efficiently and effectively. My kids work in my businesses with me, but they are not the highest-paid people in any of my companies. I am not raising my kids to think that you can just wake up and someone will give you something. That's not real life, and I want to prepare them for what the world is really like. My sons and daughters are putting in hard work and long hours. They are grinding for their paycheck. When they would come to me for money as kids, it was tied to chores and tasks. When they were in college, money was tied to grades and GPA. They start at entry-level positions with me and they work their way up, so they'll know how to do it and what it feels like to accomplish something through hard work. This is a legacy I'm leaving for them. I want them to understand how it's built from the ground up, not the top down, and to have a hands-on understanding of how the business is run and the people who run it. This way they can build a legacy for their children and teach them the same principles of hard work, responsibility, and good judgment.

Our primary focus is on empowering boys at the camp to become the next generation of leaders. An important life lesson that we give them is learning how to have greater respect for the women in their lives. This is key in building stronger communities and families. We had a young man a few years ago who was physically abusive toward his mother, and by the end of the weekend, we had encouraged him to understand just how hard she was fighting to keep him on the right track. A few months later, she shared that her son was in college and also holding down a part-time job.

One evening, we were talking about girls at the camp. This eleventh-grader stood to express himself. "Mr. Harvey, I've been friends with a girl since I was in the fifth grade and we are close. But she got this boyfriend who ain't no good. And I don't know what to do about it." Mind you, while the girl was away touring colleges, her then-boyfriend was screwing around with other girls. When the girl found out, she ran to the eleventh-grader and told him that she was going to break up with her boyfriend.

I said to the kid, "You ain't never wanted to be just her friend, have you?"

"No, sir."

"What you really want to do is kiss her?"

"Yes, sir!" And right in front of two hundred other boys, he said, "Right now!"

This little bitty dude with big glasses said, "Right now!" Everybody in the whole room started cracking up because we had all been there.

Since I had some experience and some research to share, I gave him some practical advice. I told him that he had to be there for the girl, since the other man had done her wrong. "You need to be kind to her after the other brother mistreated her. You have to offer her an alternative. Take her out somewhere. Take her to get some pizza or something. Sit down and tell her, 'Look, I know we just friends and I know this guy hurt you, but I would never hurt you. I've always wanted to be more than just your friend. I would just like for you, you don't owe me nothing right now, but to give me a chance for you to get to know me better and who I really am and see if you can like me like you like him.'" Then, I said, take her to get some coffee at Starbucks or something.

One of the camp counselors said, "Man, that's old. Mr. Harvey, girls don't drink coffee."

The smitten boy replied, "She drinks grande lattes with extra milk, with foam, and chocolate at the bottom."

The room exploded. Even the military men were high-fiving this boy. Some of his peers stood and clapped. We were impressed, because the boy had done his research for what he was hoping for. He had done his research on his girl. He didn't have the faith that he would get the girl, but he did have the hope, and he'd invested in it. We ended up giving him the nickname "Playboy" for the duration of camp.

He got that overwhelming response from his peers because he put his hope together with work. He wasn't just sitting by hoping that this young lady would magically turn into his girlfriend. He'd done his homework. He knew the exact drink she liked at Starbucks. He knew that she liked Milk Duds and popcorn with extra butter when she went to the movies. This young man was so taken by her that he noticed key things about her. If he was presented with the opportunity, he was prepared to take on the role of being considered as more than just a friend to her.

Although he may not have won that young lady's heart, he developed the skills that would endear him to another young woman. He paid close attention and knew to look for the small details of what she likes. This will permit him to eventually find another special young lady to date.

Since we opened the camp, we've mentored thousands of young men from single-mother homes from all across the country. I know firsthand that we've changed the course of these young men's lives because they tell me so all time, but, even better, they show me.

During the same camp "Playboy" attended, there was a young man who arrived with a stutter so bad that we could barely understand him. Watching him struggle with his speech took me right back to my own childhood. I struggled with stuttering until I was fifteen years old. I hated to get up in front of the class and speak. I was miserable. Kids were laughing at me. My teacher told me that they would never put someone who talked like me on television. But I never accepted that as a limitation for my life. I taught myself methods to overcome my speech condition. If I could enable this young man to overcome his stuttering, I knew he would be empowered and it would open up a whole new world for him.

I worked with him one-on-one, and started to teach him some of the methods that helped me learn. I explained to him that his biggest challenge would be in believing that he really could speak the way that he wanted to if he put in the effort and believed in himself. By the end of the weekend, I challenged him to come up to the mic, and without missing a beat, he spoke without stuttering for the first time in his life. He was able to tell the entire room that he wanted to become a writer and to be able to read his books to an audience one day. He even wrote a poem that he had composed during the week of camp. His mother was in the back of the room, and she could not contain her emotion. She could not believe it was her son standing on the stage speaking freely and clearly. He just needed to be in an environment of compassion and an understanding of the code of manhood. If I hadn't gone through that same struggle, I don't know if I would have been able to make a difference with that young man. In retrospect, I can see that going through my struggles wasn't just for me. My experiences allowed me to help this young man conquer his own challenges and see that his life was full of promise.

One of my biggest blessings is that my words of encouragement reached beyond the mentoring camp. I was offering hope and inspiration to people I had never met. I remember a chance meeting with a young man back in 2013 after my presentation at the Essence Music Festival. I had just left the stage, and I noticed a young brother was trying to get my attention. He saw me come off stage, and he ran all the way around the backstage area to meet me. He was a big guy—he was at least three hundred pounds—and was wearing a chef's coat with a food thermometer sticking out of his breast pocket. As he's running across the stage and getting closer to me, my bodyguard stepped between us, holding him back.

"I just need to holla at Steve. I have to see him today. You don't know what I've been through!" he yelled.

I saw how determined he was to get to me, and I told my bodyguard to let him through. What he said almost brought tears to my eyes. He told me that he had been incarcerated in Louisiana for five years. He had been listening to *The Steve Harvey Radio Show* since 2005. I had dedicated an entire segment of my show to inspiring inmates to restart their lives behind bars. After that show, the young man had started taking food prep classes while he was in prison. When he got out, he went back to school and continued learning culinary arts. He looked at me with tears in his eyes and said, "I just had to get back behind this stage and tell you that you changed my entire life. I'm now the head chef at the Hilton." I broke down and cried right along with him because I was so proud of what he had accomplished.

There's not a lot of hope to be found behind a prison wall. We all know how hard it is for so many former inmates to shake loose from the binds of incarceration, even once they are free. Frequently it's not about the physical bars—more often than not, it's the mental bars that are the hardest binds to break. So for this young man to make the choice to hear my voice and to change his life is beyond phenomenal. I don't know what it took for him to get up off his prison cot every day, look beyond those bars, and know that God had a greater plan for him. I can only imagine the hope it took for him to take even one step toward building his future. Even though he didn't know it, he made the decision to jump. He didn't know whether his hope would work out. He had no guarantees that his hope would carry his life beyond the expectations that were put upon it. All he knew is that there had to be something better than those prison walls. All he did was to keep pushing that hope forward until it carried him into a more positive place. And look where he is now; look where that hope got him.

Consider that many of us aren't facing the type of adversity that young man was as he listened to my show in prison. Many of us aren't facing mental or spiritual darkness as we try to find our way after being incarcerated. We take for granted all our blessings even in the face of adversity and struggle. Yet like that young man, you can use your hope to take action. He was in prison and made a jump. It shows that you can be anywhere, going through God knows what, and you can choose to take a jump. No matter what you are going though, you can change your life.

Since the camp's inception, we have changed the lives of over fifteen hundred young men. But at the same time that God rewards you with a blessing, he presents you with your next opportunity to jump. With that in mind, I started the Steve and Marjorie Harvey Foundation. Its mission is to develop programs and community-based organizations that foster excellence in our families.

Take Tyler Perry, for instance: He didn't take his stories straight to the big screen. He started out by making plays in small, local theaters in the South. In the process of learning how to act, write, direct, and produce his plays, he lost everything. He, too, lived out of his car for a while. But when he continued combining his hope with research about his passion, he made his plays stronger—with more well-rounded characters, and more layered storylines—and he tapped into a formula that has made him more successful than he knew was possible. His career is an example of putting your hope into action, and of stepping into an even greater life that God has called for you to live.

The camp started with the hope that I could help young men. When I talk about hope, I'm not talking about having a passive hope like a little kid who wakes up on Christmas morning hoping he gets everything on his list. Even with using a vision board, you can't simply put something up on a wall and hope that it will magically happen. Your dream is on your vision board as a reminder of what you want. The purpose is that subconsciously you'll do something each day to bring you closer to achieving your desires. You have to do the work. You have to make the connections. You have to be a person who is willing to take that jump before you even know what's in your parachute.

As you learn to keep your hope flexible, and to affirm yourself and your dream, your confidence will grow. This will put you in a position to take on whatever life has to give you. The young man at camp who stuttered will now reach greater heights, not because he no longer stutters, but because of his effort to overcome it. The confidence he's gained has opened his world up to more possibilities. The young brother who found out what his lady friend liked now understands the significance of researching and being prepared to work for the things in life that are important to him. The young men at the camp are all better prepared after meeting with the mentors, who have given them the foundation to be successful in any field they choose, men who have affected their lives significantly. The life lessons and skills we teach these young men go beyond how to dress for an interview, how to speak in public, or even how to network. What they ultimately learn is that they already have everything they need to be successful and to live their dreams. By being around male role models who come from neighborhoods like theirs and who have succeeded in life, they gain the confidence to believe in themselves.

As mentors, we not only advise them and nurture them, we also listen to them, which many of them sorely need. We understand where they are coming from and can relate to their struggles. Having a man to talk to can be empowering when so many of these young men have been abandoned by the men in their lives. We connect with them and help them believe in themselves, which allows them to gain the courage to overcome whatever adversity they may be facing in their lives. As these young brothers find the perseverance and resilience within themselves, they become able to believe in a brighter future, and a whole new set of doors opens.

Opening the mentoring camp with my own money was a risk I was willing to take. I had no guarantees that any of the boys would show up. I had no guarantees that I would ever get a sponsor to back our efforts. I had no guarantees I'd find the right mentors. All I knew was that I wanted to mentor young people in a formalized way. I knew that I wanted my sons to give back and be of service to young men who were not as fortunate as they were. I learned that I had friends who cared about the state of our young men just as much as I did. Giving these boys the hope that they can have a brighter future is a seed that I'm willing to plant every chance that I can get. It's an honor for me to allow

"God will do exceedingly, abundantly above all that I ask or think. Because I honor Him, His blessings will chase me down and overtake me. I will be in the right place at the right time. People will go out of their way to be good to me. I am surrounded by God's favor. This is my declaration."

other strong men to have the opportunity to give back and contribute to the lives of young men who often face huge challenges.

When you start with just a little bit of hope, you never have to ask God what the plan is for your life. You will never have to ask Him why He created you. Every morning I get up and declare these words over my life: "God will do exceedingly, abundantly above all that I ask or think. Because I honor Him, His blessings will chase me down and overtake me. I will be in the right place at the right time. People will go out of their way to be good to me. I am surrounded by God's favor. This is my declaration." I live the words every day. I believe in God's abundance for my life. I believe in God's abundance for my family. I believe in God's abundance for you.

6

Stop Existing
and
Start Living

*By facing life's challenges, you will emerge
stronger, and God will reward you by
providing you with a larger manifestation
of your dreams.*

*Accept that change is inevitable and allows
you to grow, and participate in the change.*

*Don't base your hopes on your
perceived limitations.*

*Take inventory of those in your life, and
surround yourself only with positive people.*

*Never let your past mistakes or your fears
stop you from jumping.*

I was performing in a comedy club in Memphis one
night. A stunning woman walked in. She was so
breathtaking that I almost forgot the joke I was tell-

ing. I knew she was special the moment I saw her. I pointed to her and said, "Excuse me, I know you don't know me, but one day I am going to marry you!" She laughed. "You don't know me," she said. I liked her energy off the bat. I knew right then and there that I was seriously going to marry her.

Two nights later, I saw her at another show I was doing in the same city. After my set, I asked her to come backstage and talk for a while. She told me her name was Marjorie. By the end of our talk, I could tell she was a remarkable woman. Beyond being glowingly beautiful, there was a sparkle in her eyes and a radiance to her that had me mesmerized. But what really got me was how real and down to earth she was. I loved her smile and her laugh. I thought, "This is one special lady."

After that night, Marjorie and I became fast friends and even dated on and off for a short time. Back then I was trying to make it as a comedian. Marjorie lived in Memphis and I was living out of my car, traveling city to city doing comedy gigs. I was barely making several hundred dollars a week. I didn't feel like I had anything to offer her, which is the reason I did not make a definitive move by trying to take the relationship to the next level. I was not in the emotional place I needed to be to make a relationship work. It was tough not to move forward with Marjorie, but I always kept her in my thoughts.

I focused on work as Marjorie and I went our separate ways. As time passed, I married someone else and had a son. Marjorie also married and had children. I continued to wonder about how she was doing. Every couple of years I'd call her to say hello and check on her.

More time passed. My second marriage was not going the way I would have liked. I was becoming more and more unhappy, and eventually it became clear that I had to leave my wife. I was in a dark place. I had failed at my second marriage. I was beginning to doubt if I had what it takes to make a relationship work. I felt alone and miserable. I'd even stopped listening to music, something that had always enriched my life. When I was growing up, our house was always filled with music. Sometimes we'd have spontaneous dance parties in the living room. Music was a big part of my life. At that time, I even played it for a living on the radio, but I had lost my love for it.

Leaving a marriage is always difficult. But sometimes it is necessary in order for growth. I could have stayed in a relationship that no longer supported my dreams, but I would not have been true to myself or to my spouse. If one person is unhappy in a relationship, I guarantee that the other person is, too. I was certainly not ready to make that jump, but I honestly believed that my well-being and happiness depended on it. I felt there was no way that I could become the person who God wanted me to be if I stayed.

After the jump, I was still unhappy. I felt lighter, but I was nowhere near where I wanted to be emotionally. Following a jump, you will not always believe, right away, that it was the best move. Jumping can involve nursing cuts and scrapes after you land. The only thing that kept me hopeful and faithful was my thoughts of Marjorie, which uplifted me.

One day, my longtime bodyguard suggested that I reach out to Marjorie. He knew that we'd briefly dated while I was doing a lot of stand-up. He told me, "Look, the only time I've ever seen you happy was when you were with Marjorie. Now, before you go and do something stupid and marry another woman, I'm calling her."

I still didn't think I was ready to be with a woman like her, but I recognized that my bodyguard was

---

When it comes time to make a necessary jump, you will rarely be completely ready for it. It's part of the challenge. You have to trust in God and in yourself.

---

right—she was the key to my happiness. Although I was not ready and did not feel the timing was perfect, I jumped. When it comes time to make a necessary jump, you will rarely be completely ready for it. It's part of the challenge. You have to trust in God and in yourself. We like to know what's going to happen before we take a jump, but that's not how the world works. You can't know the results until you take the action. I put it all in God's hands and jumped. Even though I felt unworthy, I swallowed my pride and reached out to Marjorie.

Two days after my divorce was final, I reunited with Marjorie. I'd lost hope of finding happiness in a relationship. She gave all that back to me. We reconnected and started dating again. It was obvious to me pretty early on that she was the woman who could help make me the man I was meant to be. Her unwavering acceptance of me, even with all my faults, enabled me to be ready to make adjustments in my life. That's part of what jumping means, being willing to embrace change. It's part of the reason we do not immediately feel elation right after a jump. Quite often, after a significant jump, we are worried, scared, and insecure about our choice. This is to be expected. It's part of the process. Change is uncomfortable, but we cannot grow without it. Although I wasn't financially ready for the move, I was more ready than I thought to make adjustments in my life. It became clear to me that I had to reconnect with Marjorie when I did, because if we'd done it sooner, I would not have been ready to show her the kind of appreciation she deserved. I wouldn't have been ready for the changes required of me to be the person I needed to be for the relationship to succeed.

We got serious pretty quickly, both of us trying to make up for lost time. You've got to be in a relationship that is not completely fulfilling to really understand what a wonderful one is. She loved me unconditionally. When we first began dating, I was just starting out in my career and was nowhere close to where I am now. I had a plan, don't get me wrong. When I first started working as a comedian, I knew, before I even told my first joke in front of an audience, that within the next five years, my goal was to become a headliner and make at least $2,500 a week. After that I wanted to up the ante and make $5,000 to $7,500 a week. But when Marjorie and I reconnected, I was making about $500 a week, if I was lucky. Marjorie told me that she didn't care how little I was making, but as a man it meant everything to me. Being able to provide for the woman in your life is one of the most important things for a man. At that time, I didn't feel I could do that. Marjorie was already established in her career. She had her own home and was providing for her family. But she made me feel comfortable with what I had to contribute financially. She respected what I had to offer and praised me for it.

Marjorie never belittled my ambitions, and she never undercut my dreams by telling me they were impossible. She always supported my endeavors and tried to inspire and motivate me to reach my goals. I knew she had my back no matter what.

A few months into dating, I was in love with Marjorie and I knew that she loved me. But, being a man, I was still connected to some women I had developed friendships with after my divorce, whom I had started casually dating. One particular night, Marjorie was visiting me in New York on Valentine's Day weekend, and one of those friends called my cell. I didn't talk much—said hi, told her we'd chat another time and that I'd stop and see her if and when I was back in town. I ended the call quickly. I didn't even think Marjorie heard the conversation—at least she wasn't acting like she did. I should have known better. She has Mom hearing; she doesn't miss a thing. Sure enough, late that night, when I got up to go to the bathroom—it was about three a.m.—there was Marjorie standing in the hallway wearing her fur coat with her suitcase in her hand.

"Where are you going?" I asked her. Her response made me realize right then and there, in the middle of the hallway, in the middle of the night, that she was the One, and if I wanted to be with her, I'd have to step up.

"I'm not trying to be anybody's plaything or anybody's woman on a string," she said matter-of-factly, her suitcase still in her hand. "I don't think you're ready for what I have to offer. I have my kids, I have a good life, and I want a man who will come in and complete my family. If this is what you want, too, I'll be in Memphis."

After I picked up my jaw, I asked her to give me one more chance. I took her bags and sat them down on the floor. I immediately found my phone and snapped it in half. I appreciated that she made it very clear what was expected of me in our relationship. I needed that kind of direct communication and structure. I knew she could help me become the man she knew I could be, by letting me know what she wouldn't put up with. I'd lost her once—this beautiful, smart, sweet woman—and I refused to lose her again. No other woman could be as loving and dedicated to me, to us, or to our children. I realized right then and there, in that hallway, that I wanted no other. Marjorie wanted a monogamous relationship—a partner who wanted to be a committed husband and father. She also needed this man to be faithful, to love God, and to be willing to do what it took to keep our family together. I jumped. I leaped toward my journey to being the man I knew she needed me to be.

I promised her that I would do anything for her and that if she stuck with me I would give her the world.

Deciding to do right by Marjorie was a jump. The jump was a personal decision to be a better person. A jump toward monogamy. A jump toward giving my whole heart to someone. It was also a commitment to myself—to live more transparently, which freed me up to consider professional options. I saw that making those kinds of decisions in your personal life can lead to greater rewards in your life overall.

When Marjorie came along, I knew that she was the right woman for me because deciding to change for her was easy. I tell women all the time: All men can change, but that doesn't mean that all men *will* change. There's only one woman whom we will change for. If a man is not willing to change, it means that you aren't the one. But you don't have to sit there and keep losing valuable years of your life with a man who's not right for you. You have to keep moving forward and believe that God has the right person for you. And not just the right person to post pictures of on social media or to show off to your girlfriends, but the right person to give you strength and encouragement to keep you jumping toward your dreams. Marjorie also knew I was the right man for her. She told me that after a few months of dating, she went to her father and said that she knew she had found the man for her. She was looking for a man who was like her father because he had set an example for her, and she said she found that in me.

There were many occasions in my life when I could have given up, stayed where I was, or resigned myself to the life I was living at the time. I could still be working at Ford or Allstate, making a paycheck but knowing I wasn't living my dream. I could have felt like a failure after flunking out of college, or seeing my friends all graduate and move on to careers without me. I could have not stepped up to be the man Marjorie needed me, that night as she stood in my hallway with her suitcase. But by facing all those challenges, I have emerged stronger. And God has rewarded me every time by providing me with a larger manifestation of my dreams. As you travel through life, you have to believe that God's plan for you is greater than any plan you could ever come up with.

As you travel through life, you have to believe that God's plan for you is greater than any plan you could ever come up with.

Marjorie and I were married in June 2007. She renewed my faith in the power of love. Her love, support, and devotion changed me in many ways. She saved me. I'm not kidding when I say that. She literally changed my life. Marjorie allowed me to stop existing and to start living. I'd never lived, I mean *really* lived, before Marjorie showed me what that meant. I truly believe that God placed Marjorie in my life to give me peace of mind and clarity. I needed her clarity. She allowed me to be clear about where I needed to go, because she gave me peace of mind. It allowed me the emotional space to think. She taught me a lot about myself. We see eye to eye on everything because what she wants, I want. We are not at cross-purposes, and she has my best interests at heart, as I have hers. I trust Marjorie implicitly.

It's not necessary to have a jumping partner, but when you do, it can be incredibly helpful. You know you have the right partner when she has the capacity to jump with you. Many of my accomplishments are because of Marjorie. I could not have made many of my jumps before I met her. Good jumping partners don't try to justify your staying put, and they don't try to hold you back or tell you that you can't do it. My wife has never talked me out of jumping. She has grabbed my hand and come with me. That's an incredible feeling when you are with the right person. She may have her hesitations about the jump, but she never tries to talk me out of jumping, because she has faith in me. Recently, I spoke with her about moving to Los Angeles. I was taping more and more television shows on the West Coast, and it made sense to live there. Mind you, I have dragged my wife all over the country, and she has made a nice home for us in Atlanta. Now, I was asking this proud Southern woman to uproot, leave it all behind, move across the country, and take the time to make a house a home. She told me that she would do whatever I needed her to do to accomplish my goals. She never ceases to amaze me.

Marjorie was the first person to tell me, "God is going to take you somewhere you've never been before, and you need to prepare for that." Her words inspire me to get up every day and work as hard as I could. Her belief in me means the world to me. And every day I want to do what I can to be a better man so that God can show me what He has in store.

On Christmas Eve 2006, I had just a few weeks before I would turn fifty. I told myself, "When I turn fifty, I'm going to reinvent myself. I'm going to get to the gym, lose some weight, and start watching what I eat." I also decided at that time to shave my head. Actually, it was a joint decision between me and Marjorie.

I started immediately, and jumped right in. I added the gym to my schedule. Concerning my eating plan, I wrapped my mind around what I could eat on my diet and did not worry about the stuff I was not supposed to eat. The bad food no longer existed in my world. Then came time to address my hair.

Maintaining my high-top fade was a big routine in my life. In order for James, my barber, to get that perfect box-cut Afro, it was an hour-long process to razor-cut it, pick it, and scissor it. When you get three or four haircuts a week, that's three or four hours of idle time when you are just sitting there. I didn't want to be married to that haircut anymore. Right before the New Year, all the hair was gone. It was a jump for me. In many ways, my hair was my security blanket. It was also what I was known for. I took pride in that hairstyle. The jump was worth it. I do not have that kind of time available in my tight schedule. By shaving my head, I now had a little extra time to be more productive or to spend with my family.

The next thing to go were my big suits. I guess Marjorie was tired of being married to a man who dressed like a pimp. It was difficult for me. Marjorie said, "Steve, you have to stop dressing like that."

"You mean to tell me that you want me to give up my suits?" I asked.

She did. "Those big pants, those long coats, and all of those buttons have to go." She explained that God had a plan for me, and I had to start dressing the part.

Throwing my suits away was another jump. I loved them. They were my signature look. I was loyal to the tailors in Cleveland, Detroit, Saint Louis, and Philadelphia who used to dress me. Urban cats loved it, and I took pride in the fact that I represented the hood well. But the suits weren't prime-time television style.

It was a critical transition for me. I had to do it little by little. I couldn't just throw the whole wardrobe away at one time. During the first season of *Family Feud*, I was still wearing the big suits. I started cycling them out until I was more comfortable in the second season with my new look. For a while I kept a few, but when I would put them back on, they didn't make me feel the same way. I didn't feel that I looked right. These changes, which may seem small to most, allowed for big changes in my life. The work started coming in steadily, and more and more opportunities came my way.

By encouraging me to make these changes, Marjorie was showing me that she was my partner in life, someone who championed and supported me. Her love gave me extra confidence that I could not only change myself, but also achieve my dreams by doing so.

Not only is change inevitable, but change allows you to grow. You can either react negatively to the change or be proactive and participate in the change. Here's the danger of reacting to change: You will always be behind. Because the change has already occurred and you're reacting to it. That will forever keep you behind, off balance, and on your heels. Or you can realize that change is inevitable, and you can be proactive and participate.

My wife helped me acclimate to our new life. Not only was she influencing my appearance, but she was also broadening my vision of the world. I had always worked hard. I was so used to working that I never really stopped to enjoy the achievements. I had money, but I had never been anywhere. Marjorie made me take time out for myself and for our family. She broadened my horizon and my scope. She suggested that we go to Paris, Morocco, Greece, Italy, Maui, and mentioned exotic locales—I hadn't even heard of some of the places she suggested we visit. She knew how to plan private, restorative vacations, which I really needed. I remember I was on a remote beach early one morning in Greece. No other people were around, and I saw a black man walking along the shore in my direction. When he got close enough, he said, "Good morning, Steve!" and kept it moving. Just like that. I was happy to see him, too, a brother on the beach on a small island off the coast of Greece, of all places, who greeted me like an old friend. He didn't even ask me for an autograph. It was a peaceful and wonderful getaway that reenergized me in ways I hadn't even thought I needed. Traveling outside my comfort zone to places I've never been, or ever considered, has broadened my worldview and has given me amazing and unforgettable moments. We've traveled all over the world because of Marjorie. All these experiences helped me grow as a man and gave me a better understanding of the world and how people are living. It showed me how blessed I am. And I know God has plenty of blessings in store for you.

What made all the difference in my relationship with Marjorie was that she was already happy. Rather than having to consume my time with making another person happy, I could focus on becoming a better person—a better husband, a better provider, and a better father. It's part of what makes our relationship work.

When Marjorie and I married, it wasn't about just the two of us. We both had children from our previous marriages. I had my children Brandi, Karli, Broderick, and Wynton; and Marjorie had her three children, Morgan, Jason, and Lori. When I became a dad to Marjorie's children, it was my honor to give them my last name. I can never take their father's place, but I'm grateful to God that I could step up and be the kind of father that they needed for this chapter of their lives. It wasn't easy trying to blend our families. Our children weren't immediately on board with our plan. And I can understand why, looking back now. They'd been on a bumpy road with me, and it's never easy to all of a sudden have a new family.

But at the time, I didn't fully understand why they felt the way they did, or why they were unhappy about it. I'm not proud of myself, but my thought was, "Look, you don't like it? Deal with it. I'm the adult, I don't need y'all's permission." Luckily, Marjorie pulled me aside and explained to me that when you're dealing with a blended family, everyone is coming from a place of broken. Just because we knew it was right, it didn't mean that our children would know it immediately. We made it clear to our kids that everyone was included in our new life. There was no *hers* or *mine*; there was only *ours*. We were a family. Whatever they didn't have before as a family, they shouldn't let that stop them from having it now.

Marjorie made my children feel they had a place they could come to and could call home. She was able to communicate our love for our children in a way that I couldn't, and she gave them a structure that benefitted them and me. What she did for my youngest son, Wynton, was such a blessing. She helped balance him in ways that I simply could not. He was far behind in school, but she dropped everything and helped turn our son into an A and B student. She gave him the attention, discipline, and encouragement he needed to focus on his schoolwork. She arranged for the necessary tutors and made him feel good about his accomplishments, which led to greater ones. As Wynton began doing better in school, his enthusiasm for it grew, and he became interested in a variety of subjects. You could practically see the newfound confidence in him. Years later, Wynton applied to colleges and got accepted into every one he applied to. He was so excited about going away to school that he nearly packed his entire room. I'm serious. He even took his fifty-six-inch flat-screen TV off the wall and tried to pack it in his suitcase! As I helped him pack, I was so proud of him and how far he'd come. When he got ready to leave, I gave him a list of seventy-five things not to do. I literally printed up a list and handed it to him at the door. A few of those things were: Stay out of jail (to do that, no stealing, no crime of any nature); don't drink and drive; and no pregnancies until he's at least thirty, and that should be when he's married. I told him that he's going to make mistakes but not to make any of the seventy-five on the list. He knows that I expect great things from him. That he should remember his name: He's a Harvey. That means something to me, and it should mean something to him.

Marjorie was instrumental in creating one big family right away. She made all our children feel included by making time for everyone. She has also been a wonderful role model for my daughters. Marjorie is a strong, smart, loving, God-fearing, and responsible woman who prioritizes family over everything else. My daughters have had a front-row seat to what that looks like, and over the years they've become impressive women themselves. Lori and Wynton left for college at the same time. Marjorie's message to Lori was to make smart decisions and to not worry about fitting in, because God made her to stand out. Marjorie has always told all our girls that they are a prize and to always be a lady. Being a lady never goes out of style.

As each of my children embarked on their higher education, I told them that I expect greatness from them. I told them the same thing that my father told me: Remember what your last name is and remember that you are my child.

My daughters have also had a front-row seat to what love looks like. They have seen me treat Marjorie with the highest level of respect. They have seen me place my wife on a pedestal and present her to the world as my queen. They've seen me lift up Marjorie higher than I have lifted myself. They've watched me take care of her. They've watched me bow down to her. They've watched me spoil her. They've watched me love and protect and honor her. By my example, my daughters know what to expect from a man; they know the ways a man is supposed to treat a woman. They know what a man who honors, respects, and cherishes a woman looks like. They have never heard me cuss out Marjorie or call her out of her name. They have seen only the highest level of respect that a man can give a woman. That has become their ideal, their personal snapshot, of what a man should do for a woman and how he should treat her.

My two daughters who are married brought home men who exemplify those characteristics. Both of my sons-in-law have said, "Man, your daughters are spoiled." To which I've said, "Thank you very much." If you come to get my daughters, and you are not into the woman-spoiling, queen-lifting, and honoring-women business, then leave my daughters alone. That's what they are accustomed to—and it's the proudest thing I've done for my daughters.

I'm not the person I used to be. It's not about me anymore. I have four full-time jobs for my children. When I'm done, I want my kids to know that somebody cared more about them than about themselves. And I want them to care more about someone else than about themselves. I love my kids, and I'm very proud to be their father. Marjorie and I have seven children. Each of them has had different challenges. Showing my sons how to jump is going to be different from showing my daughters how to jump. But my wife and I sit them down and let them know that their wings work and that we expect them to use the lessons that we have taught them to fly out and soar into their own destiny.

With Lori and Wynton at school, all of a sudden—except for my son Jason and his wife, Amanda, Karli and Morgan bringing the grandkids Noah, Benjamin, Rose, and baby Elle over—we have an empty house. I look forward to our getting together as a family and taking time off to fully enjoy it. Home for me is very special. Every summer we have a barbecue with the whole family, and every year it gets bigger and bigger with new grandchildren and a new husband or wife. My daughter Karli got married not too long ago to her husband, Ben, and my daughter Morgan had baby Elle recently. So home couldn't be any more special to me. My wife is joy. She is the happiest person I know, so when I open the door I know I will find joy and unconditional love waiting for me.

I'm man enough to say that I didn't have the right focus for my first two marriages. The demise of my marriages wasn't a reflection on the women, but those relationships showed me where I needed to grow as a man. I learned that I didn't have to base my hope on my limitations. Instead of forcing situations, I learned to let God ultimately guide me to the woman who was the right fit for me.

When Marjorie came into my life, I didn't have to force anything. God showed us how to build our relationship step-by-step. God laid out the plan for bringing our families together. Letting go of my limited hope about relationships has brought such peace and contentment into my life. I've learned from my marriage to Marjorie that I have to stay open as my life plan unfolds. I could have stayed stuck on the fact that I had two divorces behind me. But opening up my heart to Marjorie has been one of the greatest gifts in my life.

I know I wouldn't be the man I am today, where I am today, if not for Marjorie. Every great man has a woman. Now, I didn't say *successful* man; I said *great* man. Because of Coretta, Dr. Martin Luther King Jr. was able to accomplish so much more than he could have without her. And if you take Michelle out of Barack Obama's equation, you have a whole different man.

If you look at my career from 2005 to now, that's eleven years with Marjorie. The past eleven years have been the best years of my life. My life has never been this good. Although I'm still grinding every day, I've learned to leave it all at the door when I get home. I leave the workday stresses outside, and when I walk in I relax and spend time with my family. I have four new grandchildren, whom I love spending time with.

Knowing that I am not alone, that I have Marjorie in my corner, makes any load I have to bear lighter. I can depend on her. She is a great sounding board, and we often brainstorm business ideas or work through ideas I'm considering for investments together. I keep no secrets from Marjorie. Being able to unburden myself to her at the end of the day helps relieve the stresses from working long days taping back-to-back shows of *Family Feud* or of long back-to-back meetings. It's an amazing thing that happens to you when you get peace of mind. I can't put a dollar amount on peace of mind.

Marjorie helped me find inner joy and peace in myself, and that changed my relationship with my creator. Her love has allowed me to sincerely humble myself to Him and His Word. As I grew in faith, I made plans according to His path.

I started talking to Him more often. He has certainly brought me through many struggles and challenges to be the man I am today. God has given me a life far beyond anything I ever dreamed about. I know He sent me Marjorie. I cannot imagine my life without her. I could have wallowed in self-pity after my divorce was final, but I chose to participate in change. I now have the best life partner with me. I can jump higher and farther because I am jumping with her assistance. Being with Marjorie has allowed me to soar to greater heights not only personally and professionally, but also with my family. I wasn't who I wanted to be in life; my wife, Marjorie, helped me change all that. She helped me learn how to heal my relationship with my children.

For many years, my daughters Brandi and Karli didn't understand why I wasn't able to be around or spend much time with them when I first started out as a comedian. But as I grew as a person and was able to fully understand how it had affected them, and as they got older and saw how many lives I touched doing what I loved, Brandi and Karli were finally able to understand why I needed to pursue my dreams. Years later they said to me, "Dad, we didn't understand why you left us, but we know now you had to go. You didn't just belong to us. You belonged to the world." Their words and their understanding made a huge difference to me.

My family is my cocoon. The people in your cocoon, they can jump with you. They have vision and they offer a positive outlook and a positive solution. This is vital when you have a wonderful idea you want to see grow. What you need are people to tell you the best way to make that idea work. You don't need someone telling you how it *won't* work. The "how it won't work" is going to present itself as you try to make it happen. I don't need someone telling me why something won't work. I got that. I want to know what the things are we can do right now to make it work and grow into what I imagine.

My life is so busy, full, and focused now that I don't have time for fair-weather friends. I don't have time for people with a limited vision. I don't have time for people who tell me *why* something won't work. I want people in my life to tell me how to make things work; who can jump and soar with me. I have no idea when their limited vision will stop me from taking my next leap in my life. That's why I only keep people in my inner circle who I know are my biggest supporters and who will fill my life with positivity and encouragement.

Someone asked me the other day, "For a billion dollars, would you leave your wife?" and I said no. He said, "Are you kidding me, man? For a billion dollars, you could leave her and you could give her half, and still have more money than you do now." If I had the billion and lost her, where would I be? What would I do? It's not the money that makes me happy. It's Marjorie who makes me happy. It's the feeling I have when I pull up to the house. It's the feeling I have when we are sitting together while on vacation. It's the feeling I have when I'm looking at our grandchildren. It's the feeling I have when I'm making plans with her. It's the feeling I have that I can trust her 100 percent. She has my best interests at heart. She's focused on our family and is always here for us. I trust her completely and she has never let me down. I know she always has my back, no matter what. That kind of peace of mind is worth more than a billion dollars.

Don't Quit

When things go wrong, as they sometimes will,

When the road you're trudging seems all uphill,
When the funds are low and the debts are high,
And you want to smile, but you have to sigh,
When care is pressing you down a bit—
Rest if you must, but don't you quit.

Life is queer with its twists and turns,

As every one of us sometimes learns,
And many a fellow turns about
When he might have won had he stuck it out.
Don't give up though the pace seems slow—
You may succeed with another blow.

Often the goal is nearer than

It seems to a faint and faltering man;
Often the struggler has given up
Whe he might have captured the victor's cup;
And he learned too late when the night came down,
How close he was to the golden crown.

Success is failure turned inside out—

The silver tint in the clouds of doubt,
And you never can tell how close you are,
It might be near when it seems afar;
So stick to the fight when you're hardest hit—
It's when things seem worst that you must not quit

—ANONYMOUS

Acknowledgments

I would like to acknowledge my fabulous studio audience at *Family Feud* who gave the Jump speech a warm reception. I would also like to thank its 58 million viewers.

I want to thank my wife, Marjorie, for being a constant source of support, love, and encouragement in my life. These last eleven years have been the best years of my life because you have pushed me to jump higher than I ever knew that I could.

I want to thank my children—Brandi, Karli, Morgan, Broderick, Jason, Lori, and Wynton—especially my sons for providing me with the constant inspiration to jump higher and jump farther.

I thank Brandi and Dr. Steve Perry for your time and thoughts on drafts of the manuscript. My editor,

Tracy Sherrod, for her guidance and care. Leah Lakins and Carol Taylor for helping put my words on the page.

My biggest gratitude is for God, my creator. Through every jump, every leap, every fall, and every time You've allowed me to get back up and try again, You've shown me that there is nothing that You won't pull me through. And as I continue to jump, I know that there's no challenge in my life that You won't guide me through. Thank You for giving me this gift and for putting *Jump* in my imagination.

Truly Yours,
An Imperfect Soldier for Christ,
Steve Harvey

S teve Harvey is the author of the number one *New York Times* bestsellers *Act Like a Success, Think Like a Success; Act Like a Lady, Think Like a Man*; and *Straight Talk, No Chaser*. He is the recipient of multiple NAACP Image Awards and Emmy Awards. In addition to his nationally syndicated *Steve Harvey Morning Show*, Steve hosts a daily talk show on NBC and is the host of *Family Feud, Celebrity Family Feud*, and, most recently, NBC's *Little Big Shots*. The founder of the Steve and Marjorie Harvey Foundation, he lives in Atlanta, Georgia, with his wife and family.

Ready to JUMP?

Join the #JumpWithSteve *Challenge*

www.JumpWithSteve.com

Making the decision to JUMP takes courage, audacity, boldness, and faith. It requires you to take the principles, strategies, and concepts I shared in this book, and integrate them into your own life. This is how you create real, lasting change.

But that can be a challenge.

That's why I created a resource center where you can get additional insight on how to JUMP. Just go to

www.JumpWithSteve.com

and get your complimentary membership in the

#JumpWithSteve Success Club.

This free membership gives you access to my #JumpWithSteve *Challenge* as well as to other useful tools to keep you on the path to success.

It's your time. Time for you to JUMP!

HARPER LUXE

THE NEW LUXURY IN READING

We hope you enjoyed reading
our new, comfortable print size and found it
an experience you would like to repeat.

Well – you're in luck!

HarperLuxe offers the finest in fiction and
nonfiction books in this same larger print size and
paperback format. Light and easy to read, HarperLuxe
paperbacks are for book lovers who want to see
what they are reading without the strain.

For a full listing of titles and
new releases to come, please visit our website:

www.HarperLuxe.com